Conducting Student-Driven Interviews

This user-friendly book equips school practitioners with practical skills and strategies for conducting student-driven interviews—conversations that invite students of all ages to take charge of school behavior problems and build solutions based on their own strengths and resources. In contrast to traditional interviewing models that approach behavior problems by focusing on what is wrong and missing in students' lives, student-driven interviews help students discover and apply what is right and working in their lives—successes, strengths, values, and other "natural resources."

In *Conducting Student-Driven Interviews*, readers will learn how to customize every conversation one student at a time using ideas and techniques that have been field tested for application to real problems of real students in the real world of schools. The book's positive, student-driven approach is illustrated through dozens of real-life dialogues and examples involving a wide range of students and problems, and the author's irrepressible faith in students' ability to change jumps off every page. School-based professionals of all backgrounds will find *Conducting Student-Driven Interviews* an invaluable roadmap for increasing students' involvement in every aspect of their care, from goal development through evaluation of services.

CE credit is available to purchasers of this book at www.mensanapublications.com.

John J. Murphy, PhD, is a professor of psychology at the University of Central Arkansas. He is also an internationally recognized author and trainer on using strength-based therapy approaches with young people and school problems. His books have been translated into multiple languages and his work has been featured in the *New York Times* bestseller *Switch* and the training series Child Therapy with the Experts. He is a sought-after workshop presenter who has trained thousands of mental health professionals and teachers in the US and overseas. More information on his work and training workshops can be found at www.drjohnmurphy.com.

R Routledge
Taylor & Francis Group

School-Based Practice in Action Series
Series Editors
Rosemary B. Mennuti, EdD, NCSP
and
Ray W. Christner, PsyD, NCSP
Cognitive Health Solutions, LLC

This series provides school-based practitioners with concise practical guidebooks that are designed to facilitate the implementation of evidence-based programs into school settings, putting the best practices *in action*.

Assessment and Intervention for Executive Function Difficulties
George McCloskey, Lisa A. Perkins, and Bob Van Divner

Resilient Playgrounds
Beth Doll

Comprehensive Planning for Safe Learning Environments: A School Counselor's Guide to Integrating Physical and Psychological Safety—Prevention through Recovery
Melissa A. Reeves, Linda M. Kanan, Amy E. Plog

Behavioral Interventions in Schools: A Response-to-Intervention Guidebook
David M. Hulac, Joy Terrell, Odell Vining, and Joshua Bernstein

The Power of Family-School Partnering (FSP): A Practical Guide for School Mental Health Professionals and Educators
Cathy Lines, Gloria Miller, and Amanda Arthur-Stanley

Implementing Response-to-Intervention in Elementary and Secondary Schools: Procedures to Assure Scientific-Based Practices, Second Edition
Matthew K. Burns and Kimberly Gibbons

A Guide to Psychiatric Services in Schools: Understanding Roles, Treatment, and Collaboration
Shawna S. Brent

Comprehensive Children's Mental Health Services in Schools and Communities
Robyn S. Hess, Rick Jay Short, and Cynthia Hazel

Responsive School Practices to Support Lesbian, Gay, Bisexual, Transgender, and Questioning Students and Families
Emily Fisher and Kelly Kennedy

Conducting
Student-Driven Interviews

Practical Strategies for Increasing
Student Involvement and Addressing
Behavior Problems

JOHN J. MURPHY

Routledge
Taylor & Francis Group

NEW YORK AND LONDON

First published 2013
by Routledge
711 Third Avenue, New York, NY 10017

Simultaneously published in the UK
by Routledge
2 Park Square, Milton Park, Abingdon, Oxon OX14 4RN

Routledge is an imprint of the Taylor & Francis Group, an informa business

Library of Congress Cataloging in Publication Data
   Murphy, John J. (John Joseph), 1955–
   Conducting student-driven interviews :
   practical strategies for increasing student involvement and
   addressing behavior problems / John J. Murphy.—1st Edition.
   pages cm.—(School-based practice in action series)
   Includes bibliographical references and index.
   ISBN 978–0–415–63601–8 (hbk. : alk. paper)—
   ISBN 978–0–415–63602–5 (pbk. : alk. paper)
   BF637.I5M87 2013
   371.102'3—dc23
   2012032606

ISBN: 978–0–415–63601–8 (hbk)
ISBN: 978–0–415–63602–5 (pbk)
ISBN: 978–0–203–08561–5 (ebk)

Typeset in Minion
by Swales & Willis Ltd, Exeter, Devon

To the students I have been privileged to serve.
Thanks for teaching me how to be useful.

Contents

Figures, Tables and Boxes

Figures

Tables

Boxes

Series Editors' Foreword

The School-Based Practice in Action Series grew out of the coming together of our passion and commitment to the field of education and the needs of children and schools in today's world. We entered the process of developing and editing this series at two different points of our career, though both in phases of transition, with one author moving from the opening act to the main scene and the other from main scene to the final act. Despite one of us entering the peak of action and the other leaving it, we both continue to be faced with the same challenges in and visions for educating and serving children and families.

Significant transformations to the educational system, through legislation such as the No Child Left Behind Act and the reauthorization of Individuals with Disabilities Education Act (IDEA 2004), have had broad sweeping changes for the practitioners in the educational setting, and these changes will likely continue. It is imperative that, as school-based practitioners, we maintain a strong knowledge base and adjust our service delivery. To accomplish this, there is a need to understand theory and research, but it is critical that we have resources to move our empirical knowledge into the process of practice. Thus, it is our goal that the books included in the School-Based Practice in Action series, truly offer resources for readers to put directly "into action."

To accomplish this, each book in the series will offer information in a practice-friendly manner and will have a link to a website with reproducible and usable materials. These resources are designed to have a direct impact on transitioning research and knowledge into the day-to-day functions of school-based practitioners. We recognize that the implementation of programs and the changing of roles come with challenges and barriers, and as such, these may take on various forms depending on the context of the situation and the voice of the practitioner. To that end, the books of the School-Based Practice in Action series may be used in their entirety and present form for a number of practitioners; however, for others, these books will help them find new ways to move toward effective action and new possibilities. No matter which style fits your practice, we hope that these books will influence your work and professional growth.

Working with John Murphy on this important and timely project of developing ways to involve students in looking at their behavioral challenges and finding solutions has been a pleasure. In the book, *Conducting Student-Driven Interviews: Practical Strategies for Increasing Student Involvement and Addressing Behavior Problems*, Murphy provides us with a strong therapeutic foundation, basic and advanced methods on conducting student-driven interviews, and offers practical strategies for solutions. This book is comprehensive and addresses a wide variety of circumstances with students of all ages. Murphy draws upon years of experience in his work with children to provide real-life examples to demonstrate ways to individualize and personalize practical strategies for students. We are delighted to have this resource be a part of the School-Based Practice in Action Series, and we trust this will be a valuable resource for those working in schools.

Finally, we want to extend our gratitude to Ms. Anna Moore and Routledge Publishing for their support and to Dana Bliss for his vision to develop a book series focused on enriching the practice and service delivery within school settings. Their openness to meet the needs of school-based practitioners made the School-Based Practice in Action Series possible. We hope that you enjoy reading and implementing the materials in this book and the rest of the series as much as we have enjoyed working with the authors on developing these resources.

Rosemary B. Mennuti, EdD, NCSP
Ray W. Christner, PsyD, NCSP
Series Editors, School-Based Practice in Action Series

Preface

Three out of four people who talk to a helper about a problem are better off than those who don't. That's good news for those of us who spend an ample chunk of our professional lives talking with students about behavior problems. I think we can do even better at making the most of every conversation by helping students connect their unique strengths and resources to school solutions. This book offers a roadmap for doing that.

Conducting Student-Driven Interviews emerged from the requests of school practitioners and graduate students for practical strategies to engage preschool through secondary students in productive conversations about problems and solutions. Their requests can be summarized by the question, "How can we talk with students in ways that grab and hold their attention, interest, and motivation?" This book is my best shot at an answer, but the short version goes something like this: Recruit the input of students, develop goals that matter to them, and focus on what they have versus what they lack. The even shorter version boils down to two words—student involvement. Studies consistently show that the more involved people are in their own care, the better the outcomes. Research also indicates that the client–practitioner relationship as perceived by the client is the most reliable and powerful predictor of successful outcomes. This book translates these findings into practical strategies for everyday use by school psychologists, counselors, social workers, and other helpers.

Many of the book's techniques are based on the old adage that "you can't rearrange the furniture unless you're invited into the house." Unfortunately and with the best of intentions, helping professionals sometimes break down the door and start moving furniture without properly consulting the person who lives there—

especially when that person is a child or adolescent. Successful practitioners know that getting invited into a student's house requires ample amounts of respect and humility. So they listen and learn before giving advice. They customize services "one student at a time" instead of squeezing students into a one-size-fits-all model. They obtain regular feedback and adjust their approach in response to the feedback. They focus on future possibilities and have an irrepressible faith in students' strengths and resources. They are shaped into effectiveness by the people they serve.

Effective school practitioners are hopeful, respectful, change-focused, and accountable. *Conducting Student-Driven Interviews* converts these qualities into tangible skills and strategies that engage students in solution building from the opening moments of contact. Real-life examples and dialogues are used throughout the book to demonstrate practical applications with students of all ages and circumstances. In fact, every idea and technique in the book has been field-tested for application to real problems of real students in the real world of schools.

Part I begins with a collection of memorable lessons learned from the greatest teachers of all—the students themselves (Chapter 1). Chapter 2 describes the scientific, conceptual, and therapeutic foundations of student-driven interviews. A basic understanding of child and adolescent development enhances one's effectiveness in talking with young people. Chapter 3 provides an overview of school-aged development along with practical strategies for meeting students where they are and talking with them in developmentally appropriate ways.

Part II introduces the metaphor of "leading from one step behind" to capture the collaborative nature of student-driven interviews. Chapter 4 describes how summarizing, validating, and other basic skills can be applied in ways that increase student involvement and expedite school solutions. Chapter 5 presents advanced conversational skills that distinguish student-driven interviewing from other approaches.

Part III addresses the nuts and bolts of conducting student-driven interviews from getting started through maintaining positive changes. Chapter 6 provides strategies for making positive first impressions by setting a respectful and hopeful tone during the opening moments of conversation. Chapter 7 offers techniques for discussing problems in solution-focused ways, while Chapter 8 illustrates how to develop measurable goals that matter to students. Based on the research-supported idea that the most effective outcomes emerge from the student's strengths and resources, Chapters 9 and 10 provide practical ways to build solutions from students' successes, strengths, and other natural resources. Chapter 11 rounds out Part III by describing practical techniques for keeping the ball rolling in the right direction by empowering any sign of change and progress.

This book is intended primarily for school practitioners and graduate students in school psychology, counseling, social work, and other professions that serve preschool through high school students. School administrators, teachers, and parents may also find it useful in their efforts to engage young people in productive conversations. Although the book addresses students and school behavior problems, the ideas and techniques are applicable to a wide variety of populations, problems, and settings.

Speaking of other audiences and applications, the book's companion website offers a variety of resources designed to expand the book's uses and user audience. Resources include sample referral forms, classroom activities, tips for teachers and parents, and other supplementary materials for practitioners, trainees, caregivers, and students. The companion materials illustrate the broad applicability and versatility of student-driven principles and practices.

The book's title and focus is not meant to imply that talking with students is the best or only way to address behavior problems. Behavioral assessments, classroom observations, teacher and parent consultations, record reviews, and other methods are often used in conjunction with interviews to develop comprehensive interventions. This book was written for two main reasons. First, conducting therapeutic interviews with students is something that many school practitioners and trainees feel unprepared to do. Second, students are not always treated as essential partners in their own care—a troubling observation given that client participation is the key to successful therapeutic outcomes. I hope this book provides immediate and practical assistance in your efforts to involve students in the search for school solutions.

Acknowledgments

Writing a book takes time, energy, more time, support, and a little more time. Did I mention the time? For all those things—especially the time—I offer my heartiest thanks to my wife and best friend, Deb, who has provided unlimited patience, encouragement, and the occasional reminder to "get it done." To Tom, Erin, and Maura, thanks for being such reliable sources of joy and adventure over the years. To my friend and colleague, Barry Duncan, thank you for championing the cause of consumer-driven, accountable practices. I am grateful to Art Gillaspy, colleague and fellow runner, for some terrific conversations along the road. To Mara Whiteside and Lenora Nunnley, thanks for your assistance with proofreading and other tasks. To past and present students—too many to name—thank you for your energy, questions, and feedback about the work.

I want to thank all of my colleagues in the UCA Psychology and Counseling Department for their integrity and collegiality. I am also grateful for the support of editor Anna Moore and editorial assistant Sam Rosenthal of Routledge Press, and series editors Roe Mennuti and Ray Christner. To the people I have taught in classes and workshops throughout the world, thank you for your enthusiasm and ideas. Last but not least, I thank the students with whom I have been privileged to work. You are the primary inspiration for this book.

part one
Foundations

one
Lessons from the Greats

Chapter Objectives

- To portray students as the best teachers of what works and doesn't work in engaging students' attention and involvement;
- To tell four stories involving a variety of students, situations, and lessons;
- To highlight the importance of student involvement in conversations about school problems and solutions.

In the book *All I Really Need to Know I Learned in Kindergarten*, Robert Fulghum (2003) claims to have learned many of life's most important lessons—sharing, balancing work and play, and respecting others—when he was a young child in kindergarten. In that same spirit, this book could be called, *All I Needed to Know about Talking with Students I Learned from the Students Themselves*. Don't get me wrong. I have learned much from my professors and textbooks. But the best lessons of all—the ones that shook me up and got my attention and stayed with me—have come from none other than the students themselves.

Lessons from the Greatest Teachers of All

I have had the privilege of working with hundreds of preschool through high school students referred for a variety of reasons—skipping school, running around the classroom, struggling academically, cursing at teachers, bullying and being bullied, and threatening suicide, to name just a few. These students have patiently taught me what works and doesn't work in conducting interviews about school problems and solutions. Some lessons stretched across several years and involved many different students and conversations. Others sprang from a single experience and jolted me into a whole new way of approaching students; four such experiences are described below.

Rachel, Age 14

Tim Smith, the usually calm middle school principal, bursts into my office. "John, I need you on the fourth floor right now! I'll fill you in on the way." He explains that a ninth-grade student named Rachel is threatening to jump out of the restroom window and kill herself. Tim had already talked to Rachel's mother, who worked about 30 minutes away and was leaving immediately for the school. She told Tim that she and Rachel had a major disagreement that morning.

We reach the top floor. The restroom is cordoned off by several teachers to prevent anyone from entering. I gently open the door and am immediately greeted by the sound of Rachel's labored breathing. She is rocking back and forth on the window ledge—head down, eyes shut, and shivering from the cold air gusting through the window. Her breathing is fast and loud. The possibility of hyperventilation and fainting adds to the tension. Rachel turns toward me and says, "Don't mess with me or I'll jump." So begins the conversation.

"Okay, Rachel. I won't mess with you." Then, with the best of intentions, I proceed to mess with her because I am convinced that I can talk her down if I play it right. "Rachel, I know you're very upset." Before the last word leaves my mouth, Rachel shouts, "I said don't mess with me. I swear I'll jump."

"I'm sorry," I say, having struck out on my first attempt to connect with Rachel and unsure what to say next.

A minute goes by in silence save for the sounds of Rachel's heavy breathing and rocking back and forth. Then it hits me: Why should I expect Rachel to trust a total stranger and bear her soul in a situation like this? This question changes my expectations and approach.

Freed from the pressure of producing the right words at just the right time, I choose a simpler route. "Of all the people in this school, who do you most want to see right now?" This question seems to capture Rachel's attention. Her rocking and breathing slow down for a few seconds before she says, "Miss P." Miss P was short for Ms. Palumbo, a popular math teacher who had Rachel in class this semester and the year before. I crack the restroom door to tell Tim, who immediately sends for Ms. P.

Ms. P. quietly enters the restroom. Rachel is staring downward and doesn't seem to notice her arrival. At the sound of one word—"Rachel," as only Ms. P could say it—Rachel's entire body slumps and relaxes. She swings her right leg over the window ledge and onto the floor. Ms. P walks over and puts her hand on Rachel's shoulder. Rachel collapses into her arms and begins to sob—quietly at first but deeper and deeper over the next few minutes as Ms. P holds her without saying a word.

Ms. P escorted Rachel to the counselor's office, and Rachel's mother arrived a few minutes later. At some point during my 30-minute visit with Rachel, Tim had invited a local therapist to come to the school and meet with Rachel and her mother to make plans for follow-up counseling. Rachel checked in regularly with the school counselor throughout the remainder of the year. No other incidents or concerns were reported by school personnel.

Fortunately, talking students down from window ledges is not an everyday event for school practitioners. Despite the uncommon nature of this experience, however, I learned several lessons that have been useful in my everyday work with students.

Lessons from Rachel

Rachel taught me something that morning that has become a core assumption of student-driven interviewing: Every student offers a unique set of resources that can be applied toward school solutions. I call them "natural resources" because they are a natural part of students' lives—cultural traditions, family support, hobbies, resilience, and influential people such as Ms. P are but a few examples. And they are there for the asking. As I wracked my brain to come up with just the right thing to say, there was a powerful natural resource standing 200 feet away who already had what I needed from Rachel—trust, respect, and connection.

Instead of using this strategy as a last resort or by default as I did with Rachel, this book encourages you to deliberately incorporate students' natural resources into interventions and conversations with students. There is an ample body of research that supports this practice, and specific techniques for doing so are provided in Chapter 10.

Another valuable lesson I learned from Rachel is that sometimes the best thing I can do for a student is to be quiet. Putting this lesson into practice has not always been easy; I was raised Irish and we like to talk. A few seconds of silence now and then during a meeting allows us and students to process information and consider new ideas. Had I not shut up long enough to allow something different to enter my mind, I would not have thought of asking Rachel who she wanted to see.

Raymond, Age 6

Even though this story does not involve any direct contact with a student, I wanted to include it because it left such a powerful impression on me. Carol, an experienced first-grade teacher, asked me to observe a student named Raymond. "He does some things that remind me of autistic kids I've had before, and I wanted to see what you thought."

I visited Carol's classroom a couple days later and took a seat in the back of the room. She discreetly informed me that Raymond was wearing a tan-colored shirt and sitting in the first row by the windows. Carol arranged the students in small groups to work on an art assignment. I observed several noteworthy behaviors during this 20-minute activity.

Raymond repeatedly turned away from other students and looked out the window during the observation period. He twirled his hair and wiggled his pencil between his thumb and forefinger, sometimes doing so for 30 seconds or more. I recognized all of these behaviors as common among children with autism.

Disengaging from other students was a sign of social avoidance while hair twirling and pencil wiggling are forms of self-stimulation, stereotypic behavior, and perseveration.

Later that morning, Carol stopped by my office before her students returned from lunch and said, "Maybe you can come in again sometime because he didn't do much when you were there this morning." I asked what she meant and she elaborated, "I'm not saying I'm disappointed that he did better than usual, but I was hoping you could see some of the things that I've been concerned with." I didn't want to argue with her so I simply said, "Actually, I saw a few things that I think we should keep an eye on with Raymond." As I discussed the behaviors of concern that I had observed earlier, Carol's face changed from surprised to downright confused. After I finished, she asked me to walk back to the classroom with her. We stood by the door as the students filed into the classroom. Carol pointed to one of the students as he walked by and said, "That's Raymond. Who did you observe?" Ouch. When I pointed to "my Raymond" a few seconds later, Carol told me that I had observed Nathan—an academically gifted student who was being considered for placement in third grade next year. Carol explained that despite her best efforts to keep Nathan busy and challenged, he daydreamed a lot in class because he was bored.

Lessons from Raymond

Embarrassing as it was, this incident taught me a powerful lesson about expectations, facts, and interpretations. When it comes to working with students referred for school behavior problems, we often end up seeing what we are looking for. Sure, I remember taking psychology classes that addressed the self-fulfilling prophecy—the idea that we are more likely to interpret facts and events in ways that support our preheld expectations. But personal experience is the best teacher, and my encounter with Raymond and Nathan left a lasting impression on me.

When I entered the classroom that morning, I was looking for autistic-like behavior. Lo and behold, that is exactly what I saw. I have no doubt that I would have interpreted Nathan's behaviors differently had I known who I was observing. I could have just as easily viewed Nathan's window gazing as the logical result of being bored by an unchallenging task instead of seeing it as symptomatic of social disengagement and attention problems. Likewise, hair twirling and pencil wiggling may be creative strategies for staying awake rather than signs of dysfunctional, stereotypic behavior.

Yogi Berra, a former New York Yankees baseball player and coach, was arguing with an umpire when he is reported to have said, "I wouldn't have seen it if I hadn't believed it." While Yogi is known for infamous sayings that twist the language around in odd ways, my experience with Raymond suggests that Yogi may have been onto something with this one. The rule of science is that seeing is believing, but there is also some truth to Yogi's statement that believing is seeing. Social psychologists call it confirmation bias and self-fulfilling prophecy—the tendency to perceive people and events in ways that fit our preexisting theories and expectations.

I saw what I was looking for in the classroom that morning in the same way that I see what I'm looking for when I sit down to talk with a student. Our decisions about what to look for when we interview students are driven by our beliefs and expectations. The good news is that these beliefs and expectations are choices, not facts. And some beliefs are more useful than others when it comes to building school solutions. This book encourages assumptions, beliefs, and expectations that focus on what is right with students rather than what is wrong with them.

Anna, Age 17

Anna was referred to me midway through her senior year when her grades and attendance began to drop. Her teachers said that she seemed more distant, apathetic, and "not herself" in recent weeks. Anna needed to pass all of her classes in order to graduate in May, which added an extra layer of urgency to the situation.

Anna enters the office and looks around at everything except me. "Do you know why your teachers wanted us to meet?" Anna says, "Because of my grades, I guess."

"Yes, they're concerned about your grades and attendance." Anna shrugs and I add, "They said you're capable of doing the work. Is that true?" Another shrug. We plod along this way for another 30 minutes—I'm doing the heavy lifting and Anna is along for the ride, tolerating my questions and dutifully serving out her counseling sentence.

A week has passed and I decide to lay my cards on the table. "Anna, I want to apologize for last week's meeting." Anna looks puzzled. "I jumped in and started asking about your classes and grades without ever asking what *you* wanted to discuss. That was rude and I'm sorry. I want to be useful to you and to work on things that are important to you. I hope you'll give me another chance."

Anna turns away for a few seconds. When she turns back, her eyes are filled with tears. "Everybody thinks I don't care about school, but I do." I nod and she continues. "I'm going through some things now and it's hurting my schoolwork. It's hard to talk about."

I decide not to push. "Anna, what we talk about here is your choice." She takes a deep breath. "My boyfriend and I are fighting and it really bothers me. I feel like I'm going crazy. I haven't been sleeping much. It makes it hard to get to school and get my work done." I say, "No wonder it's so hard to focus on school with all this going on." Anna replies with conviction, "But I *have* to pass my classes to graduate this year." I ask what needs to happen for her to pass her classes and graduate. "I can't let these other things mess up school so much." We spend the rest of the meeting on ideas for addressing and coping with the "other things," most of which involve her boyfriend, lack of sleep, and fear of going crazy. Anna is doing the heavy lifting now.

Another week passes and Anna kicks off our third meeting by thanking me for "giving her a say" in last week's session. "My other counselors pretty much said 'here is what we're going to do' without asking me what I thought." I reply, "I really appreciate you telling me that. Speaking of last week, did you have a chance to try out any of the ideas we discussed?"

"Yes, and things have been a little better with my boyfriend. We had a long talk and that helped. Plus, I realized that if I don't look after myself, no one else will. I don't want to blow my chance of getting into college. It makes me nervous just thinking about it and maybe that's part of the problem. I get nervous about things and shut down." I say, "Is that something you'd like to work on?" Anna says yes and we spend the remainder of the meeting discussing strategies for managing nervousness. The person who barely tolerated our first session is now fully engaged in solution building.

Anna improved her school performance and attendance over the next couple weeks. Her teachers said that she was happier and on track to pass her classes as long as she kept working. I sent her a short note to congratulate her and invite her to contact me in the future if she wanted to meet again.

I didn't see Anna again until a couple months later when I called for her at the end of school year to say goodbye and wish her well. School was still going well and she met all of her graduation requirements. She had applied to two local colleges and was optimistic about being accepted. This was great news, of course, but it was Anna's parting comments that really struck me. "Thanks for helping me this year," she says.

"You're welcome, Anna. What did I do that was most helpful?" She replies, "You listened. A lot of adults don't listen. They tell you what you should do as if they know what's best for you. But you treated me like an adult instead of a kid." Anna graduated in May and began college in August.

Lessons from Anna

One lesson I learned from Anna is that students' investment in building solutions depends largely on the extent to which they are working toward personally meaningful goals—goals that matter to them. I made the mistake of assuming that Anna wanted the same thing her teachers wanted without even asking her. No wonder our first meeting flopped. It was only after I asked Anna what *she* wanted to work on that she became more involved and things started clicking. This has become a standard question that I ask all students. Student-driven interviewing involves finding out what is most important to students and tailoring school-related conversations and goals to fit their values and preferences. Chapter 8 offers other practical strategies for developing goals that matter.

Anna also taught me to admit mistakes and apologize when appropriate. When I apologized to Anna for not asking what she wanted to discuss, our relationship improved and she became more involved. I am not suggesting that we fall over ourselves apologizing to students every few minutes; just that we're willing to acknowledge our mistakes when appropriate.

Of all the lessons I learned from Anna, listening tops the list. When asked what I did that was most helpful, Anna did not hesitate in saying, "You listened." No comment about deep insights, nifty techniques, or anything like that. The simple act of listening lets young people know that we respect their ideas and experiences, and that *they* are the driving force of school solutions. These messages increase students' involvement and ownership in the change process.

As Anna said, young people are often told what to do before being asked for their ideas. Had I spent more time promoting my opinions instead of listening and asking for hers, Anna may not have told me about her negative experiences with other counselors—information that helped me avoid their mistakes and request her input on a regular basis. I now ask every student with a previous counseling experience what was most and least helpful about it, and have recently expanded the question for use with all students by asking, "In thinking about adults who have helped you, what have they done that has been most helpful?" Student-driven interviewing enhances students' involvement in their own care by listening to and asking for their ideas and feedback.

Devon, Age 9

I met Devon during my second year of practice when he was referred for intellectual and academic evaluation by his teacher, Pam. I was required to complete a social history survey on every student I evaluated, which typically took about five minutes. My experience with Devon, however, was anything but typical.

Devon enters the office and quickly takes a seat. I begin the social history survey by asking who he lives with at home. "My aunt and my five cousins," he says. I know from Devon's school file that he was removed from his mother's custody last year due to child abuse and that his father died about three years ago. When I said that I was sorry to hear about his father, Devon asked how I knew about his father. I told him about the file and he asked, "Did it say how he died?" Strange question, I thought, before replying, "No, it didn't."

Next thing I know, Devon is telling me that his father was murdered by "a guy named Gary" in the kitchen of their apartment. "They were yelling and Gary shot him," Devon says. "I ran out and then the police came. They took Gary away, and they took me to my aunt's house. That's why I live with my aunt." My quick little social history survey has taken an unexpected turn.

"I'll bet it's hard not seeing your dad," I say. Devon nods. I can barely hear him as he describes other painful experiences involving other family members. When I ask about his two older brothers, James and Robert, he tells me that James is in prison and Robert is on probation. Devon has been in three different schools during the past three years. After telling me that his aunt might move again in the summer, he covers his face with his hands and stops talking.

I had heard other painful stories from students, but this one hits me especially hard. We sit quietly for a while before I notice the tears collecting on the table under Devon's face. I finally break the silence by asking Devon what I have been thinking about for the last few minutes. "With everything that has happened to you, how do you keep hanging in there and coming to school?" Devon wipes off his face with the back of his hand and says, "My aunt tells me to never give up because quitters don't make it."

"That's interesting, Devon. What else does she do that helps?" He says, "She's always saying try hard and do your best and other things like that." He tells me that his aunt also reminds him that he could be the first one in the family to graduate from high school—a goal that is important to Devon.

I ask what else helps, and Devon describes various resources and strategies that have helped him cope with school and other challenges. I am taking notes and feeling a lot more hopeful than I did a few minutes ago. Devon also seems more engaged now that the conversation has shifted from what is wrong or missing in his life to what is available and helpful to him. He is sitting up and leaning forward. His speech has more bounce to it and he is looking more at me instead of the floor. Among other things, I learn that his brother Robert occasionally helps him with homework and that he does better in math when he is given more time to do it. I decide to end the meeting here instead of starting any testing.

I completed the evaluation a couple of weeks later, and my report included the following recommendations based on the resources I learned about in our first meeting: more homework help from his brother Robert; extra time to complete math work at school; continuation of positive messages from his aunt; and tutoring from older students at school. It was no surprise that Devon accepted these interventions and cooperated with them; they were, after all, based directly on his resources and ideas.

Devon continued to struggle academically but passed to the fourth grade. I lost touch with Devon for several years before seeing him in the hallway of the middle school. He said that school was going "okay" and that he was on the football team. Shortly after that, Devon and his family moved and left no forwarding address. I wonder if he ever met his goal of becoming the first person in the family to graduate from high school. A fuller description of Devon is available elsewhere (Murphy & Duncan, 2007).

Lessons from Devon

Devon taught me something that forms the practical foundation of this book: Every conversation is an opportunity for change. A short chat in the lunchroom, a quick question in the hallway, a social history interview—each of these provides a chance to build relationships, to increase student involvement, and to plant small seeds of change that can grow into larger solutions. The way we talk with students—our words, questions, and focus—shapes the way they see themselves and their possibilities. My conversation with Devon began with problem talk that detailed how bad things were for him without providing any direction for solutions. No wonder we felt so hopeless. As we shifted from problem talk to solution talk, a fuller and more hopeful story of Devon emerged.

Devon also taught me that problems have a way of limiting students' and practitioners' awareness of strengths, resources, and possibilities. Small successes (doing better in math when given more time), family support (encouragement from his aunt), and resilience were but a few of the resources that Devon brought to the table—resources that would have remained unnoticed had we continued to focus on what was wrong and missing in his life.

Seeking out students' natural resources is like mining for precious gems. They are not easy to see when they are buried under layers of failure and hopelessness. As it was with Devon—and as it is with many struggling students—precious resources are discovered only by deliberately digging and looking for them.

Interviewing is typically seen as an assessment tool for gathering diagnostic information, which is how my meeting with Devon began. Devon taught me that the most important goal of student interviews should be to engage students in the search for solutions. To take it a step further, interviews that are purely diagnostic and unconnected to solutions run the risk of being irrelevant and voyeuristic. This book encourages practitioners to approach every interview as a solution opportunity.

A Recap of Lessons from the Greats

Rachel, Raymond, Anna, and Devon taught me numerous lessons that drive the principles and practices of student-driven interviewing described in this book. Several such lessons are summarized below.

- Be careful what you look for because you'll probably see it (think Raymond).
- Focus on what's right vs. what's wrong with students (think Devon); conversations about strengths and resources create more hope and possibilities than conversations about weaknesses and failures.
- Students are more likely to engage in the conversation and invest in school solutions when they are working toward goals that matter to them (think Anna).
- Silence can be a good thing because it gives us and students a chance to stop and think instead of plowing forward in unhelpful directions (think Rachel and Devon).
- Listening to students strengthens the therapeutic relationship and conveys respect for their input and perceptions (think Anna); listening, like silence, can be challenging for helping professionals—especially Irish ones—because it requires us to refrain from speaking for several seconds at a time.
- Facts and interpretations are two different animals—the same set of facts or behaviors can be interpreted in vastly different ways depending on our perspective (think Raymond and Devon); interpretations are choices, not facts, so we might as well believe the best about students.
- Students are more likely to cooperate with us when we cooperate with them (think Rachel and Anna); the best way to engage students' involvement and cooperation is to make the first move by letting them know we want to be useful, inviting their input, and tailoring services to their concerns, goals, and feedback.
- Every student offers personal traits, experiences, social supports, and other "natural resources" that can be incorporated into school interventions (think Rachel and Devon); applying these resources to school solutions increases students' involvement and relieves the pressure on practitioners to create interventions from scratch.
- To err is human; to admit it can improve our relationships with students (think Anna); sure, students need to see us as competent—but competent does not mean perfect and young people appreciate adults who acknowledge their mistakes and apologize when appropriate.

■ Bonus lesson: When conducting a classroom observation, make sure to observe the right student (think Raymond); it will do wonders for your professional self-esteem and credibility.

Student Involvement: The Key to Effective School-Based Practice

As illustrated by the students in this chapter and throughout the book, there is a common thread that runs through effective interviews and school solutions. It is referred to by various names in counseling and psychotherapy circles—client involvement, participation, investment, and engagement—all of which signify the extent to which people are involved in their own care and solutions. The more involved, the better the outcome.

Think about Rachel as she straddled the window and threatened to jump. She was marginally involved until I asked who she wanted to see—a question that grabbed her attention, increased her involvement, and resulted in a solution. Anna, a polite bystander during our first session, became an active participant when she was given more of a say in the goals and content of our meetings. Devon sat up taller and talked more when the interview shifted from what was wrong and missing in his life to what was available and helpful. In each situation, stronger student involvement resulted in better outcomes.

More than anything else, this book is about involving students in their own care and solutions. The best way to promote student involvement is to include as much of the student as possible in the conversation—their words, their goals, and their resources. Active involvement occurs when students perceive the conversation, and the goal toward which it is directed, as personally relevant and worthy of their time and energy. They participate not just because they have to, but because they want to. They are emotionally involved in the conversation because it matters to them. Every idea and technique in this book is aimed at increasing student involvement—the most powerful element in student-driven interviewing.

Summary and Conclusions

Rachel, Raymond, Anna, and Devon taught me valuable lessons about how to and how not to talk with students. These "lessons from the greats" inspired me to change my entire approach. I began to focus on students' strengths and resources more than their weaknesses and problems. My outcomes improved as students became more aware of their resources and more involved in building their own solutions. Without denying or minimizing students' pain and struggles, this new way of working increased students' hope, involvement, and possibilities. For many students, their newly discovered stories of strength and competency were a refreshing change from the more familiar stories of deficiency and failure. My faith in the resiliency of students continues to grow as I watch them improve their lives in the face of major obstacles. Their heroic stories are woven into every page of this book.

Reflection and Application

1. In what ways do the lessons in this chapter differ from traditional principles and practices of interviewing students with school behavior problems?

2. Think of a situation, professional or otherwise, in which you successfully helped someone with a problem. What did you do that was most helpful? How might this be incorporated into your conversations with students referred for school behavior problems?

3. Think of two students you are currently working with, or may work with in the future, who might benefit from a conversation about what is right and what is working in their lives. What are some specific questions you might ask? Make up a few student responses and brainstorm how these responses could be further explored and incorporated into school-based interventions.

4. How do you think the interview with Devon would have developed had the conversation continued to focus on problems rather than resources? How would this have affected the development and content of interventions for Devon?

5. What are your greatest strengths and resources as a current or future practitioner? What are some specific actions you can take to build on these strengths?

6. This chapter described numerous lessons learned from a variety of students. Individually or in small groups, select one lesson and discuss its relevance and applicability to your current or future work.

two

Key Foundations and Features of Student-Driven Interviewing

Chapter Objectives

- To summarize scientific research on what works in helping people change;
- To describe the conceptual and therapeutic foundations of student-driven interviewing;
- To summarize the guiding assumptions and tasks of student-driven interviewing;
- To clarify differences between student-driven interviews and traditional interviews.

> You can't solve a problem with the same type of thinking that created it.
> —Albert Einstein

As noted in Chapter 1, lessons learned from students have strongly influenced the ideas and methods of this book. This chapter describes three other sources of influence that shape the principles and practices of student-driven interviewing:

- scientific foundations (psychotherapy research on common factors of change);
- conceptual foundations (systems theory, sociology of childhood, cultural respect and empowerment, and positive psychology); and

■ therapeutic foundations (Erickson, strategic, solution-focused, narrative, client-directed).

Findings from psychotherapy research are discussed first, followed by a discussion of conceptual and therapeutic foundations. The chapter concludes with the major assumptions and tasks of student-driven interviewing.

Scientific Foundations

Most referrals to school psychologists, school counselors, and other helping professionals are requests for change. Students typically come to us because a teacher or parent desires a change in their school performance or behavior. Our professional credibility depends largely on our ability to help people change. Psychotherapy research provides valuable hints about how to do that.

Decades of psychotherapy research have clarified the most powerful elements of change in helping relationships. This research forms the scientific basis of student-driven interviewing and helps to explain why Rachel, Anna, and Devon responded as they did in Chapter 1.

Psychotherapy Research on Common Factors of Change

Comprehensive reviews of outcome studies have led prominent researchers to propose that the success of therapy rests largely on the operation of several common factors of change (Frank & Frank, 1991; Lambert & Ogles, 2004; Wampold, 2010). The term "common factors" is used because these elements are common to successful outcomes regardless of the practitioner's specific treatment model or theoretical orientation.

Asay and Lambert (1999) proposed that effective therapeutic outcomes could be explained by four interrelated common factors. These factors are displayed in Figure 2.1 and listed below along with the percentage or extent to which each factor contributes to effective outcomes. The percentages are drawn from the work of Lambert and colleagues based on their analyses of hundreds of studies involving a wide range of clients, settings, problems, and practitioners (Asay & Lambert, 1999; Lambert & Ogles, 2004).

■ *Client factors* (accounting for 40% of change): Students' personal strengths, interests, values, life experiences, social supports, and other natural resources.
■ *Relationship factors* (accounting for 30% of change): Students' experience of respect, empathy, partnership, accommodation, and validation from the practitioner.
■ *Hope factors* (accounting for 15% of change): Positive expectancy and anticipation of change on the part of students and practitioners.
■ *Model/technique factors* (accounting for 15% of change): The practitioner's theoretical model and related techniques.

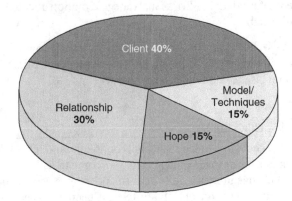

FIGURE 2.1   Common Factors of Change and Their Percentage Contribution to Successful Outcomes.

Adapted from "The Empirical Case for Common Factors in Therapy: Quantitative Findings," by T. P. Asay and M. J. Lambert (1999) in *The Heart and Soul of Change: What Works in Therapy*, by M. A. Hubble, B. L. Duncan, and S. D. Miller (Eds.), Washington, DC: American Psychological Association.

These factors are discussed below in the order of their significance and impact on building solutions.

Client Factors

Client factors represent the most potent of all ingredients in the change process. This category includes everything students bring to the table—life experiences, strengths, cultural traditions, values, special interests and talents, opinions, resilience, social support systems, and other resources.

In a recent review of research, Bohart and Tallman (2010) concluded that the client's capacity for self-healing is the most potent element in psychotherapy. Gassman and Grawe (2006) conducted a minute-by-minute analysis of 120 therapy sessions involving 30 clients, and found that focusing on clients' strengths and resources was a prerequisite of effective therapy. These findings urge practitioners to help students recognize and apply their own strengths and resources to school solutions, which is what I did with Devon in Chapter 1 after hitting a brick wall during the social history interview.

Client factors are available in every student and every situation; we just need to look for them and ask about them. I never would have learned about Devon's aunt, brother, and other important client factors in his life had I not asked about them. Unfortunately, students with problems are often viewed as having little to contribute toward solutions. In contrast to traditional interviews that focus on problems and deficiencies in people's lives, student-driven interviews actively seek out students' strengths, successes, feedback, preferences, and other client factors that can be applied toward school solutions.

Relationship Factors

The therapeutic relationship refers to the attitudes and feelings that the client and practitioner have toward each other and the manner in which they are expressed (Gelso & Carter, 1994; Norcross, 2011). Relationship factors are the second most important ingredient in the change process and include the student's experience of acceptance, empathy, respect, collaboration, validation, and encouragement from the practitioner.

Research has consistently verified the link between treatment outcomes and clients' perceptions of the therapeutic relationship (Horvath, Del Re, Flückiger, & Symonds, 2011; Orlinsky, Rønnestad, & Willutzki, 2004; Wampold, 2001). While most of the studies have involved adults, comprehensive reviews of child and adolescent therapy have verified that the relationship is equally important with young clients (Karver, Handelsman, Fields, & Bickman, 2006; Miller, Wampold, & Varhely, 2008; Shirk & Karver, 2003, 2011; Spielmans, Pasek, & McFall, 2007).

After analyzing hundreds of research studies, Orlinsky et al. (2004) concluded that the client's perception of the relationship is the best predictor of outcomes and that client involvement—referring to the client's engagement, contributions, and collaboration—is the centerpiece of a strong relationship. These conclusions verify the importance of student involvement in building school solutions as discussed in Chapter 1.

Student-driven interviewing translates research on relationship factors into practical methods such as: (a) inviting students to take an active role in shaping the goals and content of interviews and interventions; (b) obtaining their feedback on the relationship, the usefulness of our services, and progress toward their goals; and (c) adjusting services based on their feedback.

Hope Factors

Hope plays a key role in effective outcomes, though its influence is relatively smaller than that of client and relationship factors. Hope factors include students' belief that change is possible and confidence in their ability to improve school performance.

The placebo effect, a consistent and well-documented finding in drug research, attests to the power of hope in the change process. The placebo effect occurs when people who receive a sham drug or "placebo"—a pill that looks like the real thing but lacks any active chemical ingredients—feel better than people who receive nothing and often as good as those who receive the actual drug (Whalley, Hyland, & Kirsch, 2008). Placebo effects have been repeatedly observed in medicine and other forms of health care including psychotherapy (Kirsch, 2010; Price, Finniss, & Benedetti, 2008). Convincing findings on the placebo effect lead to a simple conclusion: People who expect to get better usually do.

Another important feature of hope is "self-efficacy," referring to the belief in one's ability to resolve problems and reach goals (Bandura, 2006). Self-efficacy helps students cope with frustrations and setbacks and to maintain improvements once they occur. Students who connect their achievements and improvements to their own actions are more likely to sustain such efforts in the future (Molden & Dweck, 2006). As illustrated with Devon in Chapter 1, the last thing struggling students need is a reminder of what is wrong with them; what they need is a strong dose of hope. Student-driven interviewing enhances students' hope by acknowledging their strengths and resources, focusing on future goals and possibilities, and connecting their accomplishments to their own efforts through questions such as, "What did you do differently to get your work done today?" and "How did you muster up the energy to make it happen?"

Model/Technique Factors

This category includes the practitioner's theoretical model and specific techniques associated with the model. Theoretical ideas and techniques provide useful structure and direction to the helping process; their impact on outcomes, however, is small compared to collective impact of the other common factors (Wampold, 2010).

The effectiveness of any treatment idea or method depends largely on the client's acceptance of it (Duncan, 2012), which helps to explain why no single treatment model has proven superior to others in overall effectiveness with adults (Benish, Imel, & Wampold, 2008) or children (Miller et al., 2008; Spielmans et al., 2007). These findings urge us to (a) hold lightly to our ideas and techniques instead of marrying them, and (b) tailor our approach to each student instead of fitting the student to our approach.

This discussion is not meant to bash therapy models and techniques or to minimize their value. We are continuously implementing models and techniques in the sense that everything we say and do with students (our techniques) reflects our beliefs about being helpful to them (our model). The point here is to put models and techniques in their proper perspective with other elements of change, and to use them in flexible ways based on the student's response and feedback.

Summary of Common Factors

Although the four common factors of change were discussed separately for the sake of clarity, they are highly interrelated in practice in that the enhancement of one factor strengthens other factors (Imel & Wampold, 2008). For example, students may become more optimistic about resolving a school problem (hope factor) when they are encouraged to apply their strengths and resources (client factor); or students are more likely to implement a practitioner's suggestion (model/technique factor) when they view the practitioner as respectful and caring (relationship factor). Student-driven interviewing translates psychotherapy research on common factors of change into practical strategies that help school practitioners (a) explore students' strengths and resources (client factors), (b) build cooperative partnerships with students (relationship factors), (c) instill hope for a better future (hope factors), and (d) select and apply therapeutic ideas and techniques in flexible ways that accommodate each student's preferences, resources, and feedback (model/technique factors). Additional information related to psychotherapy research on common factors can be found in Wampold (2010) and Sprenkle, Davis, and Lebow (2009).

Conceptual Foundations

This section summarizes four key conceptual foundations of student-driven interviewing—systems theory, the sociology of childhood, cultural respect and empowerment, and positive psychology.

Systems Theory: A Systemic Perspective of Schools, Students, and Problems

A system is "an entity made up of interconnected parts, with recognizable relationships that are systematically arranged to serve a perceived purpose" (Parsons & Kahn, 2005, p. 65). A school is a system comprised of students, teachers, administrators, parents, and paraprofessionals, each having different needs and levels of influence. Of all these people, students typically have the least amount of power and influence. As Parsons and Kahn (2005) noted:

> It is somewhat ironic that for most school systems ... the largest population of consumers—those for whom programs are targeted (i.e., the students attending the school)—although having a strong vested interest in the school's successful operation, may have the least influence over the school's operation. (p. 52)

One aspect of schools which students have little influence over is the referral process for counseling and intervention services. Decisions to refer students are usually made by teachers, administrators, or parents with little or no input from students. The fact that most students are "mandated clients" who come to us at someone else's request has major implications for how we approach them.

As illustrated in the following scenario, systems theory proposes that school behavior problems are embedded in a social context rather than residing strictly within the student:

> Danielle, a precocious 12-year-old, does not turn in her math homework for two days in a row. Danielle's math teacher, Ms. Jones, confronts her about the missing homework assignments. She tells Ms. Jones that she understands the work and does not benefit from homework. When Ms. Jones informs her that she is required to do homework whether she wants to or not, Danielle angrily states that "homework is stupid" and that she will do what she wants to do. Ms. Jones sends her to the principal's office, where an argument ensues between Danielle and the principal. The principal contacts Danielle's parents and recommends that she be assessed at the local counseling clinic. Danielle is diagnosed with oppositional defiant disorder and it is recommended that she receive outpatient counseling at the clinic.

Although Danielle's scenario is condensed and oversimplified, it is easy to see how social interactions can influence the development of a school problem.

From a system's perspective, a referral does not automatically imply that there is something wrong with the student. Some referrals result from a poor fit between the student and the teacher or classroom, which explains how the same student or behavior may be seen as problematic by one teacher and acceptable by another. This perspective invites practitioners to adopt a broader and more flexible view of students, problems, and solutions.

The systems perspective does not deny the reality of students' problem behavior or skill limitations, but encourages practitioners to be flexible and consider multiple pathways to school solutions—consulting with teachers and parents, altering the classroom environment, encouraging small changes in people's perceptions and actions, and building on times when the problem is absent or less noticeable are but a few options.

This book focuses on interviewing students, but that does not mean that interviewing is the best or only route to school solutions—it is simply one route. Based on the systemic notion that one small change in any aspect of the school problem can ripple into a larger solution, we can encourage students to take small steps in changing *anything* associated with the problem.

Cultural Respect and Empowerment

I wish they would only take me as I am.

—Vincent Van Gogh

Student-driven interviews encourage students to develop personally meaningful goals and to apply their strengths and resources toward reaching them. These practices fit well with the literature on cultural respect and empowerment in the helping professions. As Ridley (2005) notes: "While vigorously looking for psychopathology in ... minority clients, counselors often miss opportunities to help clients identify their assets and use these assets advantageously" (p. 103). According to Boyd-Franklin (2003), African-American clients generally benefit from strength-based approaches because they are usually more aware of their weaknesses than their strengths.

Multicultural theorists recommend a highly individualized, collaborative approach to developing therapeutic goals and selecting interventions in order to boost clients' ownership and involvement in their own care (Crethar, Torres Rivera, & Nash, 2008; Sue & Sue, 2013). Culturally alert practitioners approach every person as a unique individual regardless of his or her race, ethnicity, gender, and other cultural attributes (McAuliffe & Associates, 2013). This requires school practitioners to approach every student the same way a foreign ambassador approaches an unfamiliar country or culture—by listening before advising, by requesting people's input, by building on what already exists, and by treating people as experts on themselves (Murphy, 2008).

Cultural respect and collaboration are closely related to the concept of empowerment in schools. Dunst and colleagues (Dempsey & Dunst, 2004; Dunst, Boyd, Trivette, & Hamby, 2002) found that people experience more empowerment in participatory versus authoritarian relationships. Participatory relationships honor students' unique experiences and resources by offering suggestions in ways that accommodate their culture and perceptions, encouraging them to make use of their natural networks, and requesting their feedback.

Psychotherapy research makes it clear that client involvement is the key to effective helping relationships and positive outcomes. In other words, the person who is closest to the problem is also closest to the solution. Sadly, the prevalence of authoritarian relationships that minimize client contributions is well documented in the therapy literature (Bohart & Tallman, 2010). Student-driven interviews provide those who are closest to the problem—the students themselves—with the empowering opportunity to contribute substantially to their own solutions. As discussed next, treating young people as capable contributors is not something that comes naturally in our society.

The Sociology of Childhood: Giving Students a Voice

It's a lot better when you ask a person what they want to do.

—Molly, 10-year-old student

Sociologists have suggested that children in Western societies represent a social minority group because they are frequently viewed as impertinent and inferior. In discussing the sociology of childhood, Mayall (2002) observed that children are often seen as lacking the ability to think for themselves. Adults may, with the best of intentions, exert control in ways that stifle children's development of creativity, problem solving, responsibility, and self-confidence. From a sociological perspective, children constitute a socially disadvantaged group not just because of their age, but because of their passive position in school and society.

The points above apply to children in general, but are particularly relevant to students with a history of behavior problems. The ongoing experience of problems, coupled with society's disempowering treatment of young people, lead some students to adopt a hopeless and passive perspective on improving their school life. Student-driven conversations invite a more hopeful perspective that bolsters students' self-efficacy and involvement by: (a) acknowledging their resilience and other assets by asking how they have coped and kept things from getting worse; and (b) clarifying what is most important to them—their "big values"—and encouraging them to take small steps toward these values.

Positive Psychology

Attending to students' strengths and resources fits well with the philosophy of positive psychology, a movement that has gained progressively more attention in the helping professions (Gilman, Huebner, & Furlong, 2009; Seligman, 2011; Snyder, Lopez, & Pedrotti, 2011). In calling for a shift from psychotherapy's dominant focus on pathology to more of an emphasis on strengths and resources, Seligman, Rashid, and Parks (2006) noted:

For over 100 years, psychotherapy has been where clients go to talk about their troubles ... where the focus is nearly always on repairing negatives—symptoms, traumas, wounds, deficits, and disorders ... In its emphasis on troubles, psychology ... has seriously lagged behind in enhancing human positives ... Indeed, therapies that attend explicitly to the positives are few and far between. (pp. 774–775)

In a review of literature on child and adolescent interventions, Vera and Reese (2000) reported that young people showed greater gains in response to positive interventions that focused on their strengths and resources compared to deficit-based strategies that focused on their weaknesses and limitations. This finding rings true in my experience with students of all ages. As illustrated with Devon and Rachel in Chapter 1, the acknowledgment of positives in the lives of students does not deny the reality of their struggles and pain; it does, however, remind them that there are other aspects of themselves and their lives from which they can draw the strength, hope, and energy required to keep plugging away and trying to make things better.

Summary of Conceptual Foundations

School behavior problems do not automatically imply that students are defective or deficient as most problems are influenced by broader factors such as student-teacher relationships or classroom environments. The systemic perspective suggests that small changes in any aspect of the problem situation can ripple into larger solutions. While traditional approaches to interviewing young people reflect society's tendency to minimize their opinions and ideas, student-driven interviewing encourages students to participate in every aspect of their care from goal development through the evaluation of services. Collaborating with students to build solutions from their strengths and resources is consistent with research and best practices in multicultural counseling, empowerment, and positive psychology. These themes are reinforced in the following discussion of therapeutic foundations.

Therapeutic Foundations

Many of the principles and practices of student-driven interviewing borrow from one or more of the following therapeutic foundations: (a) the therapy of Milton Erickson; (b) brief strategic therapy; (c) solution-focused brief therapy; (d) narrative therapy; and (e) client-directed, outcome-informed practice. The major contributions of each approach are highlighted below.

The Therapy of Milton Erickson

Accept what the client offers.

—Milton Erickson

Milton Erickson is considered to be the founder of brief therapy and one of the most effective clinicians in the history of psychotherapy. Erickson died in 1980, but his contributions live on through ongoing publications and conferences devoted to studying and applying his innovative methods of helping people change.

When asked about his general theory of psychotherapy—a frequent occurrence given his remarkable success rates—Erickson would say that he had no general theory because he had never met a general client. He adapted therapy to each client instead of squeezing clients into preformed theoretical molds or treatment models. Providing services "one client at a time" is a hallmark of Erickson and a key feature of student-driven interviewing.

Erickson believed that solutions can occur without a thorough assessment and understanding of the problem. He was more interested in future possibilities than past problems. In his crystal ball technique, he invited clients to imagine a problem-free future and to describe how they had resolved their problems; when clients responded, he encouraged them to implement their own ideas. Erickson was a consummate listener and observer, alert for any hints of competency and change in his clients. He believed that small changes lead to larger and more meaningful solutions. Taking Erickson's lead, student-driven interviewing invites students to build on small steps in the right direction.

Among his many innovations, Erickson's utilization of client resources tops the list. He viewed all of his clients as inherently resourceful and resilient. Instead of giving clients something they did not already have, he encouraged them to apply their own resources toward solutions—resources that included everything from hobbies and friends to physical appearance and other personal attributes. Identifying and building on students' strengths and resources is a major feature of student-driven interviewing. Refer to Short, Erickson, and Erickson-Klein (2005) for more information about Erickson's work. His influence is evident in the approaches that follow.

The Mental Research Institute: Brief Strategic Therapy

If you keep doing what you've always done, you'll keep getting what you always got.

—Moms Mably, Comedian

Since opening its doors over 50 years ago, the Mental Research Institute (MRI) in Palo Alto, California, has been a rich source of ideas and methods associated with the brief strategic therapy model (Watzlawick, Weakland, & Fisch, 1974; Fisch, Weakland, & Segal, 1982; Fisch & Schlanger, 1999). Inspired by Erickson's conviction that change can occur rapidly even with serious problems, the MRI team videotaped and analyzed hundreds of therapy sessions with a wide range of clients and problems. The result was an intriguing theory of how problems are created and resolved (Fisch et al., 1982).

The MRI group viewed clients as stuck rather than sick; they believed that problems resulted from unproductive behaviors and social interactions rather than internal pathology. Most of the issues that brought people to the MRI began as ordinary life difficulties and grew into "problems" as the result of repetitive, unproductive solution attempts by clients and others involved in the situation. The recurring application of well-intentioned yet unsuccessful solutions made problems worse and worse—a vicious cycle that would continue indefinitely until existing solutions were replaced by different responses. The gist of MRI interventions, therefore, is to alter problem patterns and existing solutions by encouraging clients to "do something different." Students often become more empowered and willing to try something different when they view their actions as part of a problem pattern that they have some control over rather than a reflection of internal pathology over which they have little control.

Another practical feature of the MRI model is the emphasis on clarifying and accommodating the client's "position." In working with students, position consists of the student's (a) theories about the problem and solution and (b) "customership" for change, which includes the extent to which the student acknowledges the problem and is willing to do something about it. Students are more likely to accept and implement interventions that fit their positions. A student who views her teacher as mean and uncaring is not likely to accept an intervention that is presented as a way to "show more respect" for the teacher; she would be more likely to accept the intervention if it was presented as a way to "prove the teacher wrong" or "get the teacher off your case." Likewise, a student who is extremely concerned about a school problem is more likely to try an intervention that requires a high level of effort than a student who is not very concerned.

The main emphasis of the MRI approach is captured in one of the guiding principles of student-driven interviewing: If it doesn't work, try something different. The flip side of this guideline—if it works, do more of it—is the driving force of the solution-focused brief therapy approach discussed below.

The Brief Family Therapy Center: Solution-Focused Brief Therapy

> It's good to know what doesn't work, but it's really helpful to know what does.
>
> —Steve de Shazer

Solution-focused brief therapy (SFBT) was developed primarily by Steve de Shazer and Insoo Kim Berg at the Brief Family Therapy Center in Milwaukee, Wisconsin (de Shazer, 1985). SFBT has become increasingly popular due to its emphasis on efficiency, strengths, and solutions. Solution-focused therapists extended the work of Erickson by partnering with clients to develop goals and to build solutions from clients' strengths and successes. Though it began primarily as an approach for adults and families, SFBT has been successfully applied to a wide range of school behavior problems (Kelly, Kim, & Franklin, 2008; Murphy, 2008).

Repeated observations of therapy sessions led to the discovery that certain interventions were effective regardless of the client's problem. The developers of SFBT called these "formula interventions" or "skeleton keys," and shifted their focus from the lock (problem) to the key (solution). In the same way that a skeleton key opens many different locks, these interventions are applicable to a wide range of problems and continue to be used in contemporary versions of SFBT (Franklin, Trepper, Gingerich, & McCollum, 2012).

Two core interventions and skeleton keys of SFBT are the miracle question and exceptions to the problem. Inspired by Erickson's crystal ball technique, the miracle question invites clients to imagine that a miracle occurred while they were sleeping and the problem that brought them to therapy was solved, and to describe what would be different after the miracle (de Shazer, Dolan, Korman, Trepper, McCollum, & Berg, 2007). Many students enjoy the playfulness of this question and welcome the opportunity to imagine what school would be like without the problem. The miracle question often yields observable, concrete goals that can serve as guideposts for evaluating the effectiveness of services from the student's perspective. In addition to helping students develop clear goals, the miracle question boosts hope by focusing on future prospects rather than past problems.

Exceptions refer to times in which the school problem is absent or less noticeable. Based on the core guideline of SFBT—if it works, do more of it—students are encouraged to increase the frequency of exceptions or the range of settings in which they occur. Building on exceptions or "non-problems" in the lives of students draws their attention to what they are doing right—a refreshing change from the more familiar and demoralizing emphasis on what they are doing wrong.

This book owes much to the philosophy and techniques of solution-focused practice. Refer to de Shazer et al. (2007) and Franklin et al. (2012) for more information on SFBT.

Narrative Therapy

The person is not the problem; the problem is the problem.

—Michael White

Narrative therapy evolved from the work of Michael White and David Epston as originally outlined in the book, *Narrative Means to Therapeutic Ends* (White & Epston, 1990). Narrative therapists believe that we develop self-stories to make sense of our lives and that we live our lives according to these stories.

Unfortunately, many students enter services with problem-saturated stories that limit their sense of hope and self-confidence. The major goal of narrative therapy is to collaborate with clients in deconstructing problem-saturated stories and replacing them with hopeful stories that inspire solutions. Narrative therapists believe that problems persist because people come to see themselves as one and the same with their problems. This perspective leads to blame and shame, which reinforces the problem story and erodes the student's hope and self-confidence. Questions are used to reduce the grip of problem-bound stories and promote more empowering self-perceptions (How did you manage to stand up to the problem this week instead of letting it push you around? How did you come up with that idea?).

Narrative therapists often encourage clients to enlist key people in their lives to help them defeat the problem and reclaim more control of their lives. In addition to the student, "anti-problem team" members might include teachers, parents, grandparents, siblings, friends, or anyone else willing to join forces with the student against the problem. The solution-building power of influential people in a student's life was dramatically illustrated by the story of Rachel and Ms. P in Chapter 1. Student-driven conversations capitalize on the power of key people in the lives of students by identifying who they are and how they might assist the student in resolving the problem.

In discussing major attitudes of narrative therapy, Winslade and Monk (2007) highlight the importance of optimism, curiosity, collaboration, and respect for the client's wisdom and experience. These attitudes are central to the ideas and techniques in this book. Additional information on narrative therapy can be found in White (2007) and Duvall and Béres (2011).

Client-Directed, Outcome-Informed Practice

> The only man (sic) I know who behaves sensibly is my tailor; he takes my measurements anew each time he sees me. The rest go on with their old measurements and expect me to fit them.
> —George Bernard Shaw

Client-directed, outcome-informed (CDOI) practice is based on the work of Duncan, Miller, and colleagues (Duncan, 2010; Duncan, Miller, & Sparks, 2004). The developers of CDOI practice are quick to point out that it is not a model of therapy; instead they emphasize that practitioners can enhance outcomes by recruiting the client's resources and adapting services to the client's preferences, expectations, resources, and feedback. Murphy and Duncan (2007) have developed an approach to brief intervention for school problems based on the philosophy and principles of CDOI.

Seeking students' input and resources is a key feature of CDOI practice and a recurring theme throughout this chapter. Focusing on strengths and resources does not mean ignoring the student's pain and problems; rather, it requires us to acknowledge all of the stories about the student and situation—the suffering *and* the endurance; the pain *and* the coping; the struggles *and* the victories. Unfortunately, stories of weakness and deficiency often take precedence over competing stories of courage, strength, persistence, and other solution-building resources.

In their classic book, *Persuasion and Healing*, Frank and Frank (1991) note that "ideally therapists should select for each patient the therapy that accords, or can be brought to accord, with the patient's personal characteristics and view of the problem" (p. xv). This statement is every bit as relevant today as it was 20 years ago when you consider contemporary research and best practices in psychotherapy (Norcross, 2011). Psychotherapy research strongly supports the CDOI practice of tailoring services to the student's "theory of change," which includes the student's preferences and expectations related to the problem, solution, and services (Murphy & Duncan, 2007).

The use of ongoing client feedback to adjust and evaluate services is a core feature of CDOI practice. Numerous studies, including several randomized clinical trials, have shown that collecting formal, ongoing client feedback on outcome and therapeutic alliance can dramatically improve the success of services (Duncan, 2012; Lambert & Shimokawa, 2011). The developers of CDOI practice have developed short rating scales for the purpose of collecting client feedback at every session. The details of these scales, and their use with students, are discussed in Chapter 4.

Summary of Therapeutic Foundations

The therapeutic foundations of student-driven interviewing, which are summarized in Table 2.1, support the following recommendations: (a) accept and accommodate students' perceptions and goals; (b) identify and apply students' strengths, wisdom, and resources; (c) focus on future possibilities rather than past problems; and (d) invite students' participation, input, and collaboration throughout the solution-building process.

The scientific, conceptual, and therapeutic foundations in this chapter drive the major assumptions and tasks of student-driven interviewing, which are covered next.

Assumptions of Student-Driven Interviewing

Everything we do with students is influenced by our assumptions and beliefs. Assumptions guide decisions about what questions to ask, what to attend to and

TABLE 2.1   Therapeutic Foundations of Student-Driven Interviewing

Therapeutic Foundation	Key Features
Milton Erickson	View every client as unique and capable; focus on the future and on small changes; utilize whatever clients bring to therapy
Brief Strategic Therapy	Interrupt ineffective solutions; encourage something different vs. more of the same; tailor interventions to the client's position
Solution-Focused Brief Therapy	Focus on future goals vs. past problems; use "skeleton key" interventions (miracle question, exceptions) that fit a variety of problems
Narrative Therapy	The person is not the problem—the problem is the problem; externalize the problem; enlist anti-problem teams to help people stand up to the problem
Client-Directed, Outcome-Informed Practice	Treat clients as heroic contributors to their own solutions; collect client feedback on outcome and alliance; adjust services based on client feedback

what to ignore, when to talk and when to listen, and other such decisions. The story of Raymond in Chapter 1 illustrates the powerful role that assumptions play—for better or worse—in our response to students. Given that some assumptions are more useful than others when it comes to helping people change, we need to be practical and to choose assumptions based on their usefulness in promoting solutions.

The following assumptions emerge from the scientific, conceptual, and therapeutic foundations discussed earlier; each one is driven by the pragmatic goal of expediting school solutions.

Cooperation promotes change. Effective therapeutic relationships are built on mutual trust, respect, collaboration, and cooperation. Student-driven interviewing is a cooperative approach that builds strong alliances with students by treating them as collaborators and by cooperating with their opinions, preferences, and feedback. The concept of resistance has no place in this approach because students are always seen as cooperating with their own theories of change. It is our job to discover students' theories and preferences, and to structure services in ways that make sense to them and engage their involvement. If we want students to cooperate with us, we need to cooperate with them. After all, we work for them, not the other way around.

Every student offers unique "natural resources" that can be applied toward school solutions. This assumption urges us to approach each student from a fresh, hopeful perspective that honors his or her unique perceptions, resources, and circumstances. Students who struggle with serious problems often overlook their strengths, small successes, and resources. They may not even realize that they have such resources, much less apply them, unless we ask about them. Without denying the pain and frustration of serious problems, student-driven interviews invite students to acknowledge what is right and working in their lives and to apply these assets to school solutions. Viewing students as resourceful opens up solution opportunities that might otherwise remain hidden and unnoticed. Since every student brings a unique set of resources to the table, customized interventions are developed "one student at a time" based on his or her natural resources.

It is more helpful to focus on future possibilities than past problems. Unlike other approaches that spend considerable time diagnosing and discussing previous problems, student-driven interviewing focuses on small, changeable aspects of the student's future. Most students prefer to discuss what they can do to make things better rather than what they have done to make things worse. This does not mean that all discussions of the problem or the past should be avoided at all costs; to do so might invalidate the student's struggle and exclude potentially useful information. Student-driven interviewing is solution-focused, not solution-forced; it is neither problem-phobic nor past-phobic. There is a big difference, however, between discussing a problem in solution-focused ways and conducting lengthy, demoralizing investigations into the history of the problem. Whereas traditional approaches assume a logical relationship between problems and solutions, this approach assumes that solutions may have little or nothing to do with the problem. In fact, one of the quickest and simplest ways to build solutions is to increase "non-problems" or "exceptions," referring to times in the student's life when the problem is absent or less noticeable.

Small changes lead to big solutions. Big problems do not always require big solutions. The systemic idea that one small change can ripple into a larger solution is encouraging to school practitioners who have limited time to conduct elaborate interventions for every problem. Student-driven interviews invite students to take small steps toward larger solutions.

If it works, do more of it. If it doesn't work, do something different. These two statements capture the practical philosophy of student-driven interviewing. The first one emphasizes the theme of solution-focused therapy: identify what is right and what is working in the lives of students, and help them apply these strengths and resources toward solutions. The second statement urges us and students to hold lightly to our theories and techniques, and be willing to let them go and try something else when they are not working. From a practical standpoint, the value of any idea or technique rests on its practical usefulness in promoting change.

Language shapes reality. Talking with students is only one of several ways to build solutions; but it is an important one given that students are the primary focus of all school-related interventions. *What* we say and *how* we say it can shape students' perceptions of themselves and their possibilities. The wording of a question, for example, may affect not only its answer, but the way the student thinks about the topic in the future. This book encourages practitioners to use language in a mindful, deliberate way that boosts students' hope, involvement, and cooperation.

As seen in these assumptions and the tasks that follow, student-driven interviews differ from traditional interviews in several important ways. These differences are summarized in Table 2.2.

TABLE 2.2 Comparison of Traditional and Student-Driven Interviews

Traditional Interviews	Student-Driven Interviews
Focus on the student's weaknesses, deficits, and problems; problem talk	Focus on the student's strengths, resources, and solutions; solution talk
Past-focused	Future-focused
Interviewing is diagnostic; search for pathology to explain problems	Interviewing is solution-building; search for resources to build solutions
Student is viewed as "sick"	Student is viewed as "stuck"
Practitioner-driven: Goals and interventions emerge from the practitioner's model and preferences	Student-driven: Goals and interventions emerge from the student's preferences, strengths, successes, and resources
When things are stuck, student needs to adapt better to the helping process	When things are stuck, practitioner needs to adapt better to the student
Solutions result primarily from the practitioner's proper application of treatments and techniques	Solutions result primarily from the student's resources and active involvement

Tasks of Student-Driven Interviewing

Student-driven interviewing involves five major tasks as outlined below.

1. *Maintain collaborative relationships.* Nurturing and monitoring the student-practitioner relationship occurs throughout the helping process. A culture of collaboration and cooperation is created by validating students' experience and recruiting their ideas and feedback. Chapter 6 offers specific suggestions for starting off on the right foot by building positive first impressions and creating a culture of cooperation in the opening moments of contact with students.

2. *Discuss problems in solution-focused ways.* It is helpful to discuss problems in ways that acknowledge and validate students' experience while instilling hope for a better future. This involves obtaining clear descriptions of the problem, attempted solutions, and students' theories regarding the problem and solution. Chapter 7 describes strategies for talking about problems in solution-focused ways.

3. *Develop goals that matter.* Like a good compass, a clear goal provides direction and keeps the conversation on track. Student-driven interviews encourage students to think about what matters most to them and to develop specific school-related goals that support their deepest values. Strategies for partnering with students to construct useful goals are addressed in Chapter 8.

4. *Build solutions from non-problems and other natural resources.* This task builds on what is right and working for students, which includes "non-problems" (exceptions) and other available resources in their lives such as personal characteristics, special interests, and influential people. Exceptions (Chapter 9) and others resources (Chapter 10) serve as powerful building blocks for school-based interventions and solutions.

5. *Empower progress whenever it occurs.* Small improvements are empowered whenever they occur by giving students proper credit, exploring the positive consequences of improvements, and enlisting students' consultation and advice for others. Chapter 11 describes and illustrates various techniques for empowering desired changes whenever they occur in our work with students.

Student-driven interviewing is based on an interrelated set of scientific, conceptual, and therapeutic foundations as outlined in this chapter. These foundations collectively support the practice of honoring students' perspectives, preferences, and resources throughout the helping process.

Summary and Conclusions

Psychotherapy research suggests that positive outcomes in helping relationships result mostly from the operation of four common factors of change—client, relationship, hope, and model/technique factors. Student-driven interviewing activates these factors by involving students in all major decisions, developing student-driven goals, and building solutions from students' strengths and resources. Conceptual foundations include systems theory, cultural respect, the sociology of childhood, and positive psychology. This approach also borrows from the therapeutic ideas and methods of Milton Erickson, brief strategic therapy, solution-focused brief therapy, narrative therapy, and client-directed/outcome-informed practice. These scientific, conceptual, and therapeutic foundations drive the major assumptions and tasks of student-driven interviewing.

Effective interviewing requires an appreciation and accommodation of developmental factors that impact young people and school problems. Chapter 3 describes key features of child and adolescent development along with practical suggestions for interviewing students of all ages.

Reflection and Application

1. In groups of three or four, discuss your reactions to the research findings on common factors of change. You can use the following questions to facilitate your discussion: What findings surprised you the most, and why were you surprised? Which findings challenged your beliefs about what works in helping people change? What will you do differently in your work with students as a result of these findings?

2. Think of a time when you were successful in helping someone reach a goal. Reflect on this situation from a "common factors of change" perspective by addressing the following questions: Which of the common factors contributed to success in this situation? What did you do that helped to activate these factors?

3. Discuss at least one practical implication for each of the following conceptual foundations of student-driven interviewing: systems theory, the sociology of childhood, cultural respect and empowerment, and positive psychology.

4. Sociologists have suggested that children represent a social minority group in many Western societies and cultures. Is that true of your society and culture? If so, in what ways are young people treated as inferior? What impact might this have on students, schools, and behavior problems?

5. Milton Erickson focused on "one client at a time." What are the challenges of adopting this perspective in your day-to-day work with students and school problems?

6. What are two elements of the MRI's brief strategic therapy model that are particularly useful in working with students on school behavior problems?

7. Explain the concept of "skeleton keys" in solution-focused brief therapy. Think about a challenging situation involving a current or future student, and describe how one or more of the skeleton keys could be used to promote a solution.

8. In narrative therapy and client-directed/outcome-informed practice, practitioners invite clients to embrace fuller self-stories that expand their solution opportunities. What can you do in talking with struggling students to encourage fuller stories?

9. Describe how the major foundations, assumptions, and tasks of student-driven interviewing are compatible with the concepts of cultural respect and empowerment.

10. Describe one small step that you are willing to take in your work with students as a result of the information in this chapter.

three

Meeting Students Where They Are

Developmental Accommodations

Chapter Objectives

- To highlight the importance of developmental considerations in working with students;
- To describe key features of students' physical, social, psychological, and intellectual development from preschool through high school;
- To offer practical strategies for "meeting students where they are" by making developmental accommodations.

When I approach children, they inspire in me two sentiments: Tenderness for what they are, and respect for what they may become.

—Louis Pasteur

Scenario One

Jeremy, a 17-year-old student referred by his history teacher, reluctantly enters the counselor's office, slumps into the chair, and stares at the floor. When asked what he wants to work on, he says, "I don't know why I'm here. I wish everyone would get off my case and stop treating me like I'm 10 years old. Why can't they just leave me alone?"

Scenario Two

Rosa, age 6, receives special education services to improve her academic skills. Rosa's mother wants her to meet with the school psychologist (William) to address self-esteem and anger issues. William was recently assigned to the elementary school and is not very experienced talking with young children. Given Rosa's age and language limitations, William wonders what can be accomplished by meeting with her.

These scenarios provide a backdrop to this chapter's discussion of developmental factors that impact students and school problems. Basic knowledge of child and adolescent development improves our ability to communicate with students. In Scenario One, the counselor needs to tailor her approach to Jeremy's age-appropriate quest for autonomy and independence. In working with Rosa in Scenario Two, William will need to adjust his language to fit her intellectual level; he could also take a walk during the conversation to hold Rosa's attention by providing the opportunity for physical movement. These developmental accommodations help to strengthen our relationships with students by "meeting them where they are" and enhancing their involvement. This chapter highlights key features of child and adolescent development, with emphasis on their practical implications for interviewing students.

Developmental Factors

> Children are born true scientists. They spontaneously experiment and experience and reexperience again.
>
> — R. Buckminster Fuller

Some people (and credentialing agencies) think that practitioners who work with adults are automatically equipped to work with children. All you have to do is talk slower and use smaller words, right? Wrong.

Working with students requires careful attention to basic developmental tasks and preferences of children and adolescents. These issues present unique challenges *and* opportunities. The fact that most young children are playful and energetic, for example, makes it challenging to hold their attention for extended periods of time. These same attributes create opportunities to experiment with a variety of conversational formats. Talk walks and sentence completion games are two such formats that accommodate children's preference for play and action.

The remainder of this chapter describes core aspects of students' development during early childhood, middle childhood, early adolescence, and mid-adolescence. Conversational implications and strategies are provided for each phase to illustrate the link between developmental theory and practical applications. As you read through the material, remember that these are general guidelines and not specific predictions or prescriptions for individual students. There is considerable variation in the rate and manner in which development occurs among individual students. Also keep in mind that this is an overview of child and adolescent development rather than an exhaustive treatment of the topic, which can be found elsewhere (Sigelman & Rider, 2012).

Early Childhood (Ages 4–6)

Most of the people who will walk behind me will be children, so make the beat keep time with short steps.

— Hans Christian Andersen

Most children begin their formal education between ages 4 and 6, which roughly corresponds to preschool through first grade. Some students adapt easily while others struggle to adjust to the new people and expectations of the school setting. Early childhood is a time of rapid growth in physical, social, psychological, and intellectual development. These areas are discussed separately but are interdependent in the day-to-day life of a child. For example, the improvement of a 5-year-old's swimming skills can also change her self-image and peer relationships.

Physical Development

Motor skills develop quickly during early childhood, which is why most preschool programs provide ample opportunities for physical movement through activities such as printing, drawing, and playground games. The following strategies can increase young students' involvement in the conversation:

- Take a walk around the school instead of sitting in chairs.
- Have students draw a picture of the school solution and explain it.
- Keep a set of hands-on props in your office such as toys, crayons, puppets, and modeling clay.
- Conduct the interview while stacking blocks, rolling dice, assembling puzzles, or tossing a ball.
- Allow students to sit in a swivel chair that rotates (probably not a good idea for practitioners!)

Social Development

Social play is a vital part of early childhood. Children are naturally adventuresome and they appreciate adults who can and are willing to loosen up and play from time to time. Here are a few playful interviewing strategies:

- Use role-reversal activities where the student takes on the role of the helper with you in the role of the student.
- Take turns discussing what each of you like most and least about school.
- Incorporate basketball, checkers, or other games into the interview.
- Use sentence-completion, multiple choice, and fill-in-the blank methods ("I like it when my teacher …").

Some children are understandably shy at first, and these strategies help them ease into the conversation in ways that are familiar and comfortable to them.

Psychological Development

Students at this age begin to develop an identity and to distinguish themselves from others based on gender, physical characteristics, and special interests. They build self-confidence and strive for more independence. These qualities fit well with the idea of increasing students' involvement in their own care—a core goal of student-driven interviews.

Young children enjoy telling adults what they like to do and what they are good at, which can be used to develop positive interventions based on their strengths and special interests. In working with an active preschooler who loves to sing, the teacher could ask her to make up a short song every day and sing it to the class at the end of the day. This intervention might improve her behavior by acknowledging her interest in singing and increasing her involvement in the classroom.

Curiosity and imagination flourish as children become increasingly fascinated by the world. They love to experiment and make new discoveries. Some preschoolers believe in fictional characters from books, movies, and television. We can accommodate their vivid imaginations in many ways while conducting student-driven interviews. Here are a few examples:

- Ask them how their favorite cartoon character would handle the current school problem ("What would Sponge Bob do about this?").
- Have them conduct "top secret classroom experiments" in which they behave differently and observe changes in their teachers' behavior toward them.
- Invite them to direct and star in short, low-budget movies about school and school behavior ("How to Learn a Lot in School" or "How to Pay Attention in Class").

Intellectual Development

Abstract thinking is difficult for young children, so it is important to use clear, jargon-free language with them. It is often helpful to observe a parent or teacher talking with the child to see how they do it. We can also have parents or teachers sit in on the interview to facilitate communication and increase the child's comfort. Even when parents or teachers are not present, we can ask them for communication tips based on their extensive experience with the child.

Discussing the future helps young students develop goals and hopes. Given the concrete nature of their cognitive and language abilities, we need to avoid abstract language ("How will school be different one month from now when things start improving?") in favor of more playful and concrete strategies: [grabbing a coffee mug and holding it up in front of the child] "Let's pretend you rubbed this magic cup and a genie popped out and said, 'James, you have two wishes that will make school better.' What would you wish for?"

Interviewing students during the early childhood years can be challenging; it can also be quite enjoyable and productive. Any effort we make to involve the student is a step in the right direction.

Middle Childhood (Ages 7–10)

Only those who look with the eyes of children can lose themselves in the object of their wonder.

— Eberhard Arnold

Students develop many important abilities during the middle childhood years, which correspond to ages 7 through 10 and grades 1 through 5.

Physical Development

As students progress through elementary school, they develop more control and coordination of small and large muscles. Small muscle control helps with writing as well as self-care tasks such as dressing, buttoning, and tying shoes. Large muscle control affects walking, running, and throwing. Difficulties in either area can lead to school problems due to slow, inaccurate handwriting or sadness and anger about not being able to compete with peers in relay races, sports, and other playground activities.

Puberty may begin for a small percentage of children toward the end of middle childhood. Early onset of puberty can be particularly difficult for girls because they may be publicly teased during the early stages of breast development. Boys may be ridiculed when their voices begin to change. These experiences may cause embarrassment and self-criticism. Puberty can also affect the student–practitioner relationship as some children may feel uncomfortable or awkward with a practitioner of the opposite sex. Validating students' feelings and reactions goes a long way in improving their comfort level and relationship with us.

Social Development

Middle childhood is a time of considerable social activity that may involve sports, church, or neighborhood groups. Peer interaction is a major means of social development. Criticism from peers can be very hurtful to children who are seen as different or inferior, which may result in social withdrawal or aggression.

As children become more adept in social interactions and conversations, they can participate more actively in the interview process. They can also respond to questions that involve social elements:

- Who do you respect the most at school?
- What would your best friend tell you to do about this problem?
- How would another student handle this problem, and how would that work for you?
- How will your teacher treat you differently when your classroom behavior changes?

Psychological Development

While increased social awareness offers many advantages for students, it may have detrimental psychological consequences for those who view themselves as inferior to peers. Struggling students become self-critical and frustrated ("My friends are so much smarter than me, so why even try?"). Inviting students to identify small successes and competencies—a core strategy of student-driven interviewing—encourages a more empowering and hopeful outlook.

Elementary-aged students develop a stronger internal locus of control, which refers to the perception of greater personal control over their lives. Practitioners should keep this in mind when meeting with students who express hopelessness and a lack of control. For students who tell us their teachers pick on them no matter what they do, we can encourage them to change their classroom behavior and observe any related changes in their teachers' behavior. This task invites students to take responsibility for the one aspect of life over which they have some control—their own actions.

Intellectual Development

As children progress through middle childhood, they are better able to think and talk in abstract terms. They can grasp the notion of time and generalize from one situation to another. The emergence of abstract thinking also helps them empathize with the emotions and perspectives of others. All of these developments enable students to take different perspectives and consider the impact of their behavior on others ("How would you handle this if you were the teacher?"). The ability to generalize from one time to another allows students to picture how their lives will be different when things begin to improve:

- How will your teacher treat you differently next week when your behavior improves?
- How will things be different at home?
- Who will be the first person besides you to notice when things start getting better at school?

Even though elementary-aged students develop an increased capacity for abstract thought and language, it is still important to use clear and simple language. The use of toys, drawings, and other hands-on activities also facilitates communication with students in the middle childhood years.

Early Adolescence (Ages 11–14)

I'm not a kid anymore, you know.

Meagan, 13-year-old student

Early adolescence generally covers ages of 11 through 14, though it may begin a bit earlier for girls and later for boys. These ages roughly correspond to grades 6 through 8 or the "middle school" years. The transition from childhood to adolescence involves dramatic changes, especially in the psychological area. The development of personal identity and independence are vital tasks with important implications for interviewing students. Psychological development, therefore, receives the bulk of attention in the discussion of the middle school years.

Physical Development

As puberty begins and the body matures, many students become critical of their physical appearance. Rapid growth spurts and hormonal changes may diminish students' sense of control and physical coordination. These changes can also be confusing and upsetting to students because they are accompanied by new sexual feelings, thoughts, and insecurities.

Similar to previous stages, the developmental domains of early adolescence are interdependent in that changes in one area influence other areas. Physical changes and appearance, for example, can strongly impact a middle school student's self-identity, confidence, and social relationships.

Social Development

The influence of peers and the desire for social acceptance continues to grow during this time. Adolescents may feel as if everyone is looking at them, especially when they make mistakes or embarrass themselves in school or other public places. Striking a balance between fitting in with peers and carving out a personal identity is an ongoing challenge of adolescence.

As illustrated with Rachel and Devon in Chapter 1, identifying people with social influence in the student's life expands intervention and solution opportunities. In some cases, for example, a respected peer or family member can be called upon to provide valuable support and advice to the student. Tapping into the power of social relationships is a respectful and developmentally appropriate way to work with middle school students.

Knowledge of social development is also helpful in working with parents and teachers. Factual information about development may help them understand that some problem behavior is influenced by normal processes of development. For example, when a student's misbehavior is seen as partly motivated by a strong desire for peer attention, it normalizes the situation and reduces the likelihood that parents or teachers will view the student as emotionally or behaviorally disturbed. Likewise, parents may feel hurt or angry when their child spends less time with them or occasionally questions their authority. Explaining to these parents that their child is displaying a common and healthy transition from childhood to adolescence helps them better understand and cope with these changes.

Psychological Development

The physical and hormonal developments of early adolescence, coupled with sexually oriented thoughts and feelings that often accompany them, may increase students' anxiety, shame, and self-consciousness. Given the increasing importance of physical appearance and social approval, it is not surprising that a student's self-esteem may bounce up and down a lot during middle school. Sudden and dramatic mood swings are also common and may prompt confusion, anger, and defiance. Some students view mood swings as a sign that they are "going crazy," which is not an unusual thought at this age. We can normalize student's experience by explaining that sudden mood changes are a scary yet common experience during adolescence and beyond. (Welcome to life!)

Adolescents may also engage in magical thinking and perceptions of invincibility. It is common, for example, for students to believe that bad things can happen to other people but not them—a belief that increases their risk-taking behavior in school and other places.

Ironically, the times when struggling students most need understanding from adults are the times they receive it the least. This occurs because (a) adolescents may not discuss their problems with adults because they don't want to be criticized or lectured, and (b) the student's defiant behaviors drive people away instead of bringing them closer. Some students become suspicious and distrustful of adults in general. Nonjudgmental listening—a key skill of student-driven practice—helps to gain adolescents' trust and involvement in the change process (Martin, Romas, Medford, Leffert, & Hatcher, 2006).

Student-driven interviewing is well suited to the psychological struggles and preferences of middle school students. Complimenting students on their strengths, for example, helps to counteract the effects of self-criticism and shame. In discussing the benefits of strength-based approaches with young people, Wolin, Desetta, and Hefner (2000) encourage practitioners to "look for strengths in even the most troubled young people and encourage them to search for examples of their own competence" (p. 4).

Intellectual Development

The adolescent's increased ability to think and speak in abstract terms permits more sophisticated conversations involving the following types of future-oriented and "what if" questions:

- If this problem vanished in two months, how would your life be different at school?
- What would happen if you tried that in class tomorrow?
- How would it change things between you and your parents?
- What would Mr. Porter do if you walked into class tomorrow and thanked him for being your teacher? How willing are you to do that?

These questions capitalize on students' growing intellectual skills and quest for independence by inviting them to describe what they want in the future and what they are willing to do to make it happen. Students often have more influence on their school experience than they think. Student-driven conversations invite them to envision a better school experience and take concrete action toward pursuing it.

Mid-Adolescence (Ages 15–18)

If you cheat them when they're children they'll make you pay when they're sixteen or seventeen by revolting against you.

—John Lennon

The developmental changes of early adolescence are extended and refined during mid-adolescence, which corresponds to ages 15 through 18 and grades 9 through 12 of high school.

Physical Development

Physical development generally involves the continuation or completion of changes that began in early adolescence. Many females achieve full breast growth during mid-adolescence. Males typically acquire facial hair and their voices become deeper.

Concerns about physical appearance continue through the high school years. Not surprisingly, major difficulties in physical development—or noticeable physical differences between a student and his or her peers—can strongly affect the student's social status, identity, and self-esteem.

Social Development

Peers take on more importance and influence during mid-adolescence than any of the previous stages of development. Dating and sexual relationships may occur, and students develop stronger gender identifications. Mid-adolescence can be a time of anguish and peer rejection for students who experience gender confusion and those who embrace sexual orientations that differ from the dominant majority (McGuinness, 2008). Once again, listening and validating the experience of all students helps to establish respectful and productive therapeutic relationships.

Whereas friendships during early adolescence are often linked to common connections such as sports or living in the same neighborhood, high school friendships are based on deeper and more personal factors such as values and social compatibility. As a result, friendships usually become more enduring and stable during the high school years. All of these factors influence students' school performance and response to practitioners. The fact that student-driven interviewing invites students to develop personally meaningful goals fits well with the increased emphasis that adolescents place on personal values during the high school years.

Psychological Development

The turbulence of early adolescence is gradually replaced by more enduring and stable patterns of thinking, feeling, and acting. The journey toward increased stability, however, is not a smooth and easy one for many high school students. Students test out different roles and behaviors. Sexual activity and drug use increase. As students move through high school, they are faced with stressful decisions about their future. The excitement of increased freedom is often coupled with apprehension and self-doubt as illustrated by questions such as "What if I make the wrong choice?" or "Is this what I really want to do?" For many students, this is their first realization that big decisions often involve angst and conflict.

Increased privileges, such as driving a car and scheduling one's own time, are accompanied by more responsibilities. The balance of freedom and responsibility is a source of major conflict for many teenagers and their caregivers. From a parent's or teacher's perspective, it may seem like the student wants the freedom but is unwilling to accept the responsibility that comes with it. From the student's perspective, parents and teachers seem unwilling to provide the freedom required for the student to become responsible.

Of all the issues facing adolescents, the pursuit of independence and identity is often the most important one to bear in mind when talking with high school students. In the process of developing a distinct and personal identity separate from parents and friends, adolescents go to great lengths to preserve and assert their independence and freedom. Comments such as, "It's my life, not yours," and "I know what's best for me," are common at this age. Parents usually hear these statements more than anyone else. Students' quest for independence, however, is relevant to school practitioners and others who work with them on school-related problems. High school students resent it when adults question their freedom to think for themselves, which is why it is so counterproductive to try to talk them out of their opinions and into ours.

The collaborative philosophy of student-driven interviewing accommodates adolescents' fierce commitment to freedom and independence. Cooperating with students' perspectives and preferences helps to avoid power struggles and reinforces the notion that students are accountable for their opinions, decisions, and outcomes. Students are more likely to engage and cooperate with us when their opinions are heard and respected. This point was firmly made by Anna in Chapter 1 when I asked what was most helpful about our meetings and she said: "You listened. A lot of adults don't listen. They tell you what you should do as if they know what's best for you. But you treated me like an adult instead of a kid."

Intellectual Development

Adolescents can engage in increasingly complex discussions as their intellect expands through the high school years. Students' ability to consider different perspectives enables them to respond to more complex questions such as:

- How would you respond if you were the teacher/parent?
- What would your teacher say if I asked for his ideas about resolving this problem?
- What would your grandfather do if he was facing this problem?

High school students' growing ability to visualize and reflect on their hopes and possibilities provides opportunities to explore what they want from our services and for their future ("Imagine that it is one month from now and that our meetings have worked well. How would you know that the meetings were successful? What would be different at school? What did you do to help make that happen? What did I do that helped you the most?").

Appendix A provides an overview of the developmental features and accommodations described in this chapter. Developmental issues affect students in a variety of ways from preschool through high school. Basic knowledge of child and adolescent development allows us to adjust our approach to students of all ages. I urge you to keep these developmental issues in mind throughout the remainder of the book.

Summary and Conclusions

This chapter summarizes developmental factors that influence students from preschool through high school, along with their practical implications for interviewing students. Key features of physical, social, psychological, and intellectual growth were described for four phases of development: early childhood, late childhood, early adolescence, and mid-adolescence. Practical implications and accommodations were provided for each phase. Developmental accommodations serve to strengthen the most important ingredient of all in student-driven interviewing—student involvement. The next two chapters build on these accommodations by describing the major skills involved in conducting student-driven interviews.

Reflection and Application

1. How does a practitioner's basic knowledge of child and adolescent development help in working with students and school problems?
2. Describe one strategy that you could use to elicit young people's ideas for solutions when working with students in each of the following stages: (a) early childhood; (b) middle childhood; (c) early adolescence; (d) mid-adolescence.
3. Interviewing preschool and kindergarten students can be challenging because of their limited intellectual and language abilities. Describe two interviewing techniques for communicating with and sustaining the attention of children in the early childhood stage of development.
4. Play is an important activity for many children. How can we tap into children's natural enjoyment of play and adventure during school-related interviews?
5. Some students become more suspicious and distrustful of adults during the adolescent years. Explain how the use of compliments and nonjudgmental listening are helpful in working with students in middle and high school.
6. The vigorous pursuit of independence and identity is a major task of adolescence. Describe two interviewing strategies that demonstrate respect for adolescents' quest for independence.
7. Describe one small step that you are willing to take in your work with students as a result of the information in this chapter.

part two
Skills

four
Leading from One Step Behind

I: Basic Interviewing Skills

Chapter Objectives

- To offer the concept of "leading from one step behind" as a guiding metaphor for student-driven interviewing;
- To describe and illustrate the basic skills of student-driven interviewing—listening, allowing for silence, attending to nonverbal behavior, summarizing, paraphrasing, validating, flexibility and playfulness, and collecting feedback.

> In the beginner's mind, there are many possibilities, but in the expert's there are few.
>
> —Shunryu Suzuki

Student-driven practice involves "leading from one step behind" (Cantwell & Holmes, 1994). That has a nice ring to it, but what exactly does it mean to lead from one step behind? The short answer goes something like this: It means actively leading the conversation by asking useful questions, encouraging student involvement, and structuring services based on the student's goals, resources, and feedback. The "one step behind" part means trusting that students know themselves and their experiences better than we do and allowing them to teach us what they want from life and school (their goals), what they already know and have that is helpful to them (their wisdom and resources), and how we can be most useful in helping them reach their goals (their preferences and feedback).

Basic Skills in Conducting Student-Driven Interviews

This is the first of two chapters that describe and illustrate specific skills involved in leading from one step behind. This chapter covers eight basic interviewing skills that lay the groundwork for positive relationships and school solutions. Many of these skills are common to other approaches but are applied in a unique way in student-driven interviewing.

Listening

> What people really need is a good listening to.
>
> —Mary Lou Casey

Listening may be the most important skill of all in working with students. In meeting with focus groups comprised of students with major learning and behavior problems, I always ask, "What can adults do to be most helpful to you?" Listening often tops the list. As illustrated with Anna in Chapter 1, listening increases students' involvement in building solutions and lets them know that we respect their perceptions and contributions.

Student-driven interviewing involves (a) listening without judging and (b) listening for any hints of resilience, hope, and other resources. Uninvited evaluations and judgments shift the focus of conversation from the student to the practitioner, causing students to focus more energy on defending their positions than building solutions. Listening with a non-evaluative ear creates a safe environment in which students can be open and honest without the fear of being judged.

Effective listening also requires us to be alert for clues about students' strengths, successes, and other resources. As Egan (2010) points out:

> If you listen only for problems, you will end up talking mainly about problems. And you will shortchange your clients. Every client has something going for him or her. Your job is to spot clients' resources and help them invest these resources in managing problem situations and opportunities. (p. 146)

Allowing for Silence

> It's the silence between the notes that makes the music.
>
> —Zen Proverb

Allowing for silence does not come naturally to many practitioners, especially those from Western cultures where action is the rule and silence is the exception. Silence is often viewed as a sign of discomfort, and it can be unnerving for practitioners who pressure themselves to keep the conversation going at all costs. But students may see things differently. For a confused or anxious student, for example, silence provides a much-needed opportunity to reflect on the conversation and sort out thoughts. As noted in Box 4.1, some questions require more reflection than others. We need to let students know that silence is okay, and to validate their silence with comments such as "It's a really hard question" and "Take as much time as you need."

Box 4.1 Big Questions, Big Silences

Consider the following questions as they apply to you and your life:

1. What do you want your life to stand for?
2. What is most important to you?
3. What are you willing to do next week to move closer to your goals?

These are important questions, and we need to provide students with adequate periods of silence to reflect on them before answering. Big questions often require big silences.

If we jump in and break up every silence after only a few seconds, students may feel rushed or forced to talk even when they don't know what to say or would prefer to say nothing at all. When this happens, the interview turns into a superficial game of verbal tennis where the practitioner serves up a question, the student returns the answer, and so on. Rapid-fire conversations of this nature rarely produce solutions.

There are times when long periods of silence are not productive. In the early moments of the first interview, for example, students may benefit from our help in keeping the conversation going. For students with speech and language problems, long silences may cause anxiety or embarrassment. Developmental factors also influence the function of silence for individual students. Young children are often warned about talking to strangers. Adolescents may be suspicious and guarded during the first session. Some students have never experienced sitting in front of an adult who provided sustained and undivided attention for more than a few minutes at a time. In these situations, it is generally not helpful to allow long periods of silence.

Efficiency is important, but that does not mean that students are rushed into solutions by impatient practitioners who view silence as wasted time. As indicated above, the timely and respectful use of silence can be very helpful at certain points in the conversation.

Attending to Nonverbal Behavior

Nonverbal behavior provides clues about people's feelings and perceptions, but we need to be cautious in interpreting such behavior—especially when we are working with students whose cultural backgrounds and mannerisms are different from our own. With this cautionary point in mind, this section discusses various aspects of practitioners' and students' nonverbal behavior.

The Practitioner's Nonverbal Behavior

Students are very good at reading us to determine our genuineness and engagement in the conversation. Egan's (2010) SOLER model describes five areas of nonverbal behavior for practitioners to consider when meeting with students. These are general guidelines that need to be adapted to each student.

S: Face the student. Facing the student indicates involvement and attention. Direct facing intimidates some students, so it might be better to adopt a more diagonal or angled position. Sitting fairly close to the student also communicates interest and involvement, though it should not be so close as to invade the student's personal space and cause discomfort.

O: Open posture. An open posture conveys accessibility and involvement, whereas the crossing of arms or legs may signal less involvement. Once again, this is a general guideline and not a rule. If you are more comfortable sitting with your legs crossed, then you should probably do that. I occasionally "mirror" the student's posture and other nonverbal behaviors as long as doing so is not perceived as disrespectful or disingenuous; I might, for example, slouch in my chair a bit if the student is slouching or lean in when the student leans in.

L: Lean toward the student. In many cultures, leaning forward and closer to someone is a sign of interest and respect, whereas leaning back says, "I'm not with you" or "I'm bored." Leaning too far forward may be awkward for some students. I find myself leaning forward when students talk about their perceptions and successes. I might also lean forward to catch a student's gaze if they look down a lot, being careful not to alarm them or force the issue. Occasional head nods and changes in facial expression also communicate our active involvement in the conversation.

E: Eye contact. Eye contact conveys our interest and attention. This is not to suggest that we should constantly look at the student, which causes discomfort because it is more like staring than attending. As with the other nonverbal behaviors, cultural factors influence students' views of eye contact. In some cultures, children are discouraged from making eye contact when speaking to adults because it shows a lack of respect for the adult.

R: Relaxed approach. Students are more likely to relax when we relax as indicated by our facial expressions, posture, and speech. Unusual facial expressions, hurried speech, fiddling with our hands, or tapping our feet can distract students and reduce our credibility.

Before ending this section, I want to comment on another behavior that I often observe in supervising students and others: smiling. Occasional smiling communicates our acceptance and caring. However, smiling for prolonged periods or at inappropriate times comes off as phony and insincere. For example, smiling as a student describes a personal concern may be seen as a sign that we are not listening or that we do not care.

The Student's Nonverbal Behavior

The nonverbal behavior of children generally is more transparent than that of adults as they are less sophisticated in concealing their thoughts and feelings. (Perhaps it would be a better world if we were all so unsophisticated.)

Students' nonverbal behavior helps us assess their reactions to our questions and comments. Smiling, frowning, nodding, lowering their voice, shifting in their chair—all of these behaviors provide hints about how students are doing during the conversation. The actual meaning of a particular behavior for an individual student depends on the student's unique style and the context in which the behavior occurs—for example, in response to a particular question or topic. Even when we consider these factors, we still need to be cautious about reading too much into students' nonverbal behavior. When a behavior strikes us as important, we can always check with the student to guard against misinterpretation:

- Your eyes opened up and your voice got a little louder when you answered that question. Why do you think that is?
- You looked down more when you were talking about your older brother. What do you make of that?
- Is this important for us to talk about, or would you rather talk about something else?

The subtle nature of body language makes it difficult to pick up on students' nonverbal behavior let alone our own. One way to sharpen our awareness of nonverbal behavior is to periodically videotape an interview or ask a colleague to observe. We can also ask ourselves the following questions right after an interview (adapted from Egan, 2010, p. 136):

- What are my attitudes toward this student?
- How would I rate the quality of my presence with the student on a scale of 1 (very low) to 10 (very high)? What can I do next time to increase this number?
- To what degree does my outer behavior reflect my attitudes and thoughts about the student and situation?
- In what ways am I distracted or prevented from giving my full attention to the student?

Summarizing

Summarizing serves the following purposes in student-driven interviewing: (a) clarifying major themes and staying on track; (b) inviting students to elaborate on their experiences; and (c) validating students' perceptions and feelings. Summarizing is defined as periodically restating the student's feelings or perceptions in a condensed, non-evaluative way.

After listening to Reggie describe why he misbehaves in history class, we might say: "So, the biggest reason you act up in history class is because you hate history and you're bored. Is that correct or is there something else?" In keeping with the cooperative tone of student-driven interviewing, this summary includes Reggie's own words and invites him to revise or add to it as needed. The following exchange with a 14-year-old student named Kim further illustrates the respectful use of summarizing.

Kim:	Mr. Henderson [the teacher] doesn't like me. It's been this way all year. He's always picking on me in class.
School Practitioner (SP):	He's always picking on you? [Inviting elaboration by echoing the student's words.]

Kim:	All the time. No matter what I do, I always get in trouble in that class. Even when I turn in my homework, I still get in trouble for something stupid.
SP:	Something stupid like …? [Echoing again to encourage elaboration.]
Kim:	I might laugh at something my friends say. Mr. Henderson will look over and see us laughing, and I'm the one who gets in trouble.
SP:	So you feel picked on because you're the one who gets in trouble for doing small things even when other students are involved. Is that it or is there something else? [Offering a summary and inviting Kim to accept, amend, or reject it.]
Kim:	Yes.
SP:	Okay. You're in a very tough situation, aren't you? [Reflecting Kim's feelings of frustration.]

As illustrated with Kim, effective summaries are descriptive rather than interpretive and are offered in a way that allows students to modify them as needed. Summarizing can also help us shift from problem talk to solution talk. Consider the following dialogue from the opening moments of the second session with Laura, age 9, who was referred by her math teacher (Ms. Beck) for disruptive classroom behavior. During the first meeting, Laura talked at length about her frustration with Ms. Beck and her math class.

School Practitioner (SP):	Laura, I was wondering what's better at school since we talked a few days ago.
Laura:	You know how I was telling you about Ms. Beck and how mean she is.
SP:	Yes.
Laura:	Well, she's still doing it. My brother said she was the same way when he was in her class a couple years ago. She expects everybody to be perfect little angels. But I'm not like that, so I get sent to the principal a lot.
SP:	You get sent to the principal a lot from Ms. Beck's class? [Using Laura's own words to summarize her position.]
Laura:	She sends me there all the time and it's boring because I just sit there and wait for the principal. He's always busy so he can't see me right away.
SP:	That sounds boring just sitting there waiting for the principal. [Acknowledging Laura's frustration.]
Laura:	Believe me, it is.
SP:	So you would rather be somewhere else?
Laura:	Yes.

SP: Where would you rather be instead? [Asking Laura instead of making assumptions or suggestions about where she would rather be.]

Laura: In class with my friends.

SP: So you would rather be in class with your friends, but you keep getting sent out and having to sit and wait in the principal's office. I wonder what you could do differently to stay in class more with your friends. What do you think? [Summarizing Laura's position while inviting her to focus on solutions.]

Summarizing can also be used at the end of an interview to restate students' goals, offer compliments, and suggest homework tasks. The following statement was made at the close of the first meeting with Raul, an 11-year-old student referred for minimal work completion.

SP: We've covered a lot of ground today, and I'd like to go over a few things to make sure I understand what you want and what we talked about. Is that okay?

Raul: Sure.

SP: You want to become an important and good man. [Using Raul's words to restate his long-term goal.] To do that, you'll need to do better in school by doing more work in class. [Restating the short-term goal.] I think it's great that you know what kind of person you want to be and that you're willing to do more work at school to make it happen. [Validating Raul's goals and complimenting him on his commitment to improve.] You're already doing some of this in spelling, and it's going to take hard work to do it in math and reading. [Acknowledging his success in spelling and noting that change often requires hard work.] You seem like a brave guy who likes challenges and doesn't give up easily, so it will be interesting to see how things go for you this week. [Acknowledging his strength and encouraging him to stay with it.] You can keep track of how you're doing on the little card we talked about. [Reminding Raul of a simple self-monitoring strategy we discussed to help him maintain his focus between sessions and track his progress toward the goal.] Okay?

Raul: Okay.

SP: Do you have any questions?

Raul: No.

SP: I enjoyed talking with you today, Raul, and I'll check with you in a few days to see how things are going with the card and the schoolwork.

This discussion has focused on the practitioner's use of summarizing, but we can also ask students to summarize when appropriate. In addition to giving students a chance to revisit key themes of the conversation and ensuring that they are involved in the conversation, having them occasionally summarize key themes reinforces their pivotal role in the change process.

Paraphrasing

Paraphrasing serves similar purposes as summarizing—clarifying students' comments and perceptions, encouraging them to elaborate, and laying the groundwork for solution talk. In paraphrasing, the practitioner reflects the content of the student's communication in shorter form, often immediately following the student's comment. Paraphrases are used more than summaries because they are shorter and cover a smaller chunk of the conversation.

Ivey and Ivey (2008) recommend the following steps in constructing a paraphrase:

- A sentence stem (*So you are saying that ...*)
- Inclusion of the student's key words (*... you're going to do "what you want to do" ...*)
- The essence of what the student said (*... because it's your life.*)
- An accuracy check (*Is that right?*).

The following is an example of paraphrasing with Monique, a 9-year-old student who complained about the difficultly and amount of math homework.

Monique:	I have trouble with math homework. Sometimes I don't know how to do it. There's a whole bunch of it every night. I can't get it all done because my mom works at night so she can't help me.
SP:	So math homework is hard to get done because there's a bunch of it and your mom is not there to help you.
Monique:	Yes.
SP:	Tell me about a time when you got your math homework done, or when you got a little more of it done than you usually do.

Paraphrasing, like summarizing, enhances our relationship with students by letting them know that we are listening and taking them seriously.

Validating

In graduate school, I took a class from a respected professor and psychotherapist named Dr. Kelly. Of the many insights and stories he shared, nothing was more memorable than what he told us on the last day of class. It started with a question from one of the students: "If you could offer just one piece of advice to beginning therapists, what would it be?" Dr. Kelly thought about it for few seconds and answered in one word: "Validation." He elaborated by sharing a few research findings and clinical experiences that demonstrated the importance of validation. Then he surprised us all by discussing his personal experience as a therapy client: "Of all the insights and strategies I experienced, the most healing part of all was the therapist's validation that I was a worthwhile human being. And you know what? That alone was worth all the time and money I put into it." Dr. Kelly ended class with a simple piece of advice: "If you do nothing else for your clients, make sure to affirm and validate them because they are probably doing the best they can at any given moment." I will never forget this statement and I hope that Dr. Kelly's advice is evident throughout this book and, more importantly, to the students I serve.

In student-driven conversations, validation involves: (a) Listening to what students say and how they say it; (b) accepting their feelings and perceptions at face value; (c) normalizing their concerns and struggles; (d) acknowledging their desire to change; and (e) partnering with them to construct interventions that complement their perceptions, goals, and resources. It is obvious from this list that validation draws on various interviewing skills. The opportunity to tell one's story to an accepting listener is a powerful experience for students. Summarizing and paraphrasing allow students to "hear themselves" and to find validation in doing so. All of these strategies encourage students to reflect and elaborate on their perceptions, which can lead to new insights and behaviors.

Methods of validation can be subtle or direct. Subtle forms of validation, referred to as "minimal encouragers" (Meier & Davis, 2011), include responses such as "yes," "sure," "okay," "of course," and "uh-huh." The following examples are more direct and specific forms of validation:

- I can see why it's so important for you to stand up for yourself instead of backing down.
- No wonder you're so anxious—it's a big decision and you need to consider your options before deciding.
- It makes perfect sense to take your time instead of rushing in and trying to fix this all at once.
- It's understandable to feel that way with everything you've been through lately. I'm wondering how you've managed to hang in there without giving up.

"Normalizing" is a specific type of validation that accepts and normalizes students' perceptions instead of evaluating them. When students feel judged or criticized, they may become defensive and go to great lengths to justify their position—time and energy that would be better spent on building solutions. Solving problems is hard enough without having to defend oneself in the process. Normalizing removes the need to defend or justify, which enables students to focus more intently on resolving the problem at hand.

One situation in which normalizing is especially helpful is when students fear that they are "going crazy" in response to ongoing problems or unwanted thoughts and feelings. Consider Gabriella, a 17-year-old student referred by her art teacher due to sudden changes in her mood and behavior. Her art teacher became concerned when Gabriella began acting "different from her usual self"—showing up late for art class, making rude comments to the teacher and peers, and leaving class without permission two days in a row.

Gabriella arrived at the first meeting looking tired and troubled. She shared these comments later in the session:

> My boyfriend told me he wanted to break up last week after being together for about a year. I'm pretty depressed about it. Everybody tells me that he's not worth it and to get over it and move on. But we were together for

a whole year and I still care about him. My friends tell me about other guys who I could go out with, and they're always saying things like, "He's not the only fish in the ocean." But I don't want anybody else. I know I should get over it, but I can't. I don't know what's wrong with me. I cry all the time and I feel like I'm flipping out. I haven't been eating like I should and it's affecting my schoolwork, but I don't feel like doing anything except sleeping and crying.

Normalizing begins by listening to, accepting, and validating students' experiences without judgment or evaluation ("Breakups can be so tough. No wonder you feel so upset and scared."). Many students experience immediate relief when they are able to share their concerns with a nonjudgmental listener. Normalizing also requires us to refrain from verbal or nonverbal behaviors that convey surprise or criticism, such as frowning or asking why students feel the way they do.

Humor can help provide relief and normalize students' experience if—and it's a big if—it is done in a respectful and tactful manner. Many students enter services with a grim and hopeless perspective that dampens their energy and creativity. When used appropriately, humor can loosen the problem's grip and free students up to consider creative solutions. Consider the following dialogue with Gabriella.

School Practitioner (SP):	So your friends are trying to get you to go out with other guys by saying things like, "He's not the only fish in the ocean."
Gabriella:	Yes.
SP:	But you haven't been fishing anywhere for over a year, right?
Gabriella:	Right.
SP:	They're telling you to head for the ocean, and you haven't even fished in a small pond or lake for an entire year. No wonder this is so frustrating for you. Do you even remember how to cast a fishing pole at this point?
Gabriella:	Kind of [smiles a little]. But I don't want to right now.
SP:	That's understandable. It's your decision, not someone else's. A lot of people would advise against jumping from one big relationship into another right away.
Gabriella:	That's what I told my mom and my friends.
SP:	Yes. It sounds like they really care about you and want you to be happy. But you want to make your own decisions for yourself when you are ready to make them.
Gabriella:	That's right.

Gabriella accepted the fishing metaphor, which may have provided some relief, validation, and hope. I want to share a few thoughts before leaving the topic of humor. First, humor should always serve the student, and should never be used to meet our desire to be funny. Second, we need to be cautious about saying anything that patronizes students or invalidates their pain and distress. The benefit of a humorous comment never outweighs the risk of damaging the relationship. A final rule of thumb about using humor with students: If you have any reservations about using it in a particular situation, then you probably shouldn't.

Validating students' feelings and perceptions does not require practitioners to agree with them. Our job is to help students resolve problems, not to convert them to our way of thinking. Validation frees students from defending themselves and allows them to focus their attention and energy on building solutions.

Flexibility and Playfulness

At the risk of stating the obvious, working with young people requires a willingness to be flexible and playful. We can be sitting on the floor with a restless preschooler one hour and meeting with a sullen teenager the next. As discussed in Chapter 3, our effectiveness depends partly on our flexibility in adapting our approach to the student's age, abilities, and preferences.

Flexibility and playfulness go hand in hand. Most young people are playful and they respond well to lively and playful practitioners. Here are a few interviewing tips and strategies that tap into students' playfulness:

- Have students draw a picture of the solution and explain it to you.
- Keep sessions short, take occasional breaks, and have "walk talks."
- Have students take you on a tour of the school and talk about their classes as they walk by the rooms.
- Sit on the floor and let students sit in the "big chair."
- Have students teach you something at the start of every meeting.
- Conduct a portion of the interview in "bounce talk" using a basketball or tennis ball, where we bounce the ball to the student when we ask a question or say something and vice versa ["How did you get your work done this morning?" (bounce); "I just made up my mind to do it" (bounce); and so forth].
- Play a variation of the "20 Questions" game where students think of the best solution to the school problem, then you ask questions aimed at figuring out their solution.

Being flexible and playful can strengthen the therapeutic relationship by tailoring the conversation to the student's style and preferences.

Collecting Feedback

Shouldn't I be telling you what I think?

—Molly, 10-year-old counseling client

The most accurate way to monitor and improve our services is to obtain regular feedback from the people we serve. Research indicates that: (a) clients and practitioners often differ in their perceptions of the therapy process (Lambert, 2008; Tryon, Collins, & Felleman, 2006); (b) clients are more accurate than practitioners in evaluating and predicting the outcome of services (Kazdin, Marciano, & Whitley, 2005; Lambert, 2008); (c) practitioners grossly overestimate their effectiveness and fail to see poor outcomes in the making (Hannan et al., 2005); and (d) clients' early experience of change and of the therapeutic relationship are strongly predictive of eventual outcomes (Lambert & Shimokawa, 2011; Zuroff & Blatt, 2006). These findings, in conjunction with the empirical link between client involvement and treatment outcomes (Orlinsky et al., 2004), make a strong case for obtaining student feedback and adjusting services based on their feedback.

This section describes practical strategies for monitoring students' perceptions of progress (outcome feedback) and the student-practitioner relationship (alliance feedback). Similar feedback can be obtained from teachers, parents, and others who are involved with the student. Student feedback can be obtained through formal rating scales or informal scaling questions. We'll start with informal strategies.

Informal Scaling Questions

Practitioners can ask the following scaling question at every meeting to assess the student's perception of progress: "On a scale of 0 to 10, with 0 being 'the worst it can be' and 10 'the best it can be,' how would you rate the school problem/goal during the past week?" It is helpful to remind students that there is no right or wrong answer and that the purpose of the question is to obtain their honest view of progress. Inviting students to explain their responses helps us understand what the ratings mean to them ("You rated things 3 points higher last week. What's changed at school to make things worse this week?").

Similar questions can be used to find out what students think about the relationship and the usefulness of our services: "On a scale of 1 to 10, with 1 being 'really low' and 10 being 'really high,' how would you rate our connection so far?"; "On a scale from 0 to 100, how helpful was today's meeting?" We also need to follow up on these questions to determine what we can do to improve the relationship ("What can I do differently to be more helpful? What can we do next time to make the meeting even more useful?"). The next section describes two formal, practical tools for obtaining student feedback during interviews.

Formal Rating Scales

Collecting formal client feedback on outcome and alliance has been shown to dramatically improve the outcomes of therapy (Duncan, 2012; Gillaspy & Murphy, 2012; Lambert, 2010). Among the validated client feedback measures that can be used with children and adolescents, two rating scales stand out for their practicality—the Outcome Rating Scale (ORS; Miller & Duncan, 2000) and Session Rating Scale (SRS; Johnson, Miller, & Duncan, 2000). Each measure contains only four items and takes less than a minute to complete. The ORS is administered at the beginning of every session and the SRS is administered at the end. Both measures are displayed in Appendix B along with their child versions for students 5 to 12 years old—the Child Outcome Rating Scale (CORS, Duncan, Miller, & Sparks, 2003) and Child Session Rating Scale (CSRS, Duncan, Miller, Sparks, & Johnson, 2003). The use of the ORS and SRS at every session has consistently improved outcomes with a variety of clients (Anker, Duncan, & Sparks, 2009; Miller, Duncan, Brown, Sorrell, & Chalk, 2006; Reese, Nosworthy, & Rowlands, 2009).

These ultrabrief rating scales gather client feedback on research-identified elements of outcome (ORS) and alliance (SRS). Positive changes in the areas assessed on the ORS—personal distress, interpersonal well-being, social relationships, and overall well-being—are considered to be valid indicators of successful outcomes (Miller, Duncan, Brown, Sparks, & Claud, 2003). The SRS taps into students' perceptions of the practitioner's respect and understanding, the relevance of goals and topics covered in the session, and the student-practitioner fit—all of which impact the therapeutic alliance.

The ORS and SRS use a visual analog format of four 10-centimeter lines, with instructions to place a mark on each line with low estimates to the left and high estimates to the right. The four 10-centimeter lines add to a total score of 40. The total score is the sum of the marks made by the client to the nearest millimeter on each of the four lines, measured by a centimeter ruler or template. Items can be read aloud to students who have difficulty reading independently. When parents and teachers are involved, they should complete the same outcome scale given to the student. For example, if the student completes the CORS, then the parent and teacher would also complete the CORS. Having multiple raters allows for comparison and exploration of similarities and differences among people's ratings ("Scott, I noticed that you rated the school scale a lot higher than your science teacher did. What do you make of that?").

The usefulness of these measures depends almost entirely on the quality of discussion that accompanies them. The numbers alone mean nothing without the explanation behind them—that is, without knowing what they mean to the student. These tools can become an integral part of the conversation that allows students to actively participate in building solutions. Additional tips and scripts for using these measures in schools can be found in Appendix C. The ORS and SRS are available in several languages and are free for individual use from www.heartandsoulofchange.com.

Obtaining feedback from students lets them know that we value their input and that we are willing to adjust services based on what they tell us. Feedback enables us to detect and correct problems in our work with students before the problems reach a point of no return. As Kazdin (2007) states: "Now that measures are available … their use ought to be strongly encouraged in clinical training and practice" (p. 44).

There is a convincing body of research that supports the practice of collecting feedback; besides that, it just seems like common courtesy to invite those for whom a service is designed to have a role in evaluating and shaping that service. Table 4.1 summarizes this and other basic skills involved in student-driven interviewing.

TABLE 4.1 Basic Skills of Student-Driven Interviewing

Skill	Description	Example
Listening	Listening without judging; listening for hints of resilience, hope, and other resources	Student says, "I've always had trouble in school," which is a sign of resilience
Allowing for silence	Permitting yourself and students the opportunity to occasionally pause and reflect in silence	Saying "take your time" after asking a thought-provoking question; explaining that you need a minute to think about things
Attending to nonverbal behavior	Being mindful of students' and your own behavior nonverbal behavior; exercising caution and cultural sensitivity in interpreting such behavior	Using eye contact, open posture, and other SOLER behaviors that convey interest in students and their perceptions
Summarizing	Restating students' stories or perceptions in a condensed, non-evaluative way	Summarizing a student's lengthy story about various struggles in middle and high school by saying, "It sounds like school has been very tough on you for several years. Is that true?"
Paraphrasing	Rephrasing students' comments in shorter form; similar to summarizing but involves shorter segments of the conversation	Student: "My parents talk and talk, but they never bother to listen to me or ask what I think about anything." Practitioner: "You want your parents to respect your opinions more."
Validating	Accepting and affirming students' perceptions and experiences at face value	Telling a student, "No wonder you're so anxious and upset about this."
Flexibility and playfulness	Adapt your approach in playful ways based on the student's age, abilities, and preferences	Sitting on the floor with a preschooler; taking a walk; using hands-on props
Collecting feedback	Monitoring students' perceptions of progress and alliance on a regular basis using informal or formal scaling methods	Asking, "On a scale of 0 (really bad) to 10 (really good), how did school go this week?"; Having students complete the ORS and SRS at the beginning and end of every meeting

Summary and Conclusions

This chapter describes eight basic interviewing skills for leading from one step behind and laying the groundwork for solutions: listening, allowing for silence, attending to nonverbal behavior, summarizing, paraphrasing, validating, flexibility and playfulness, and collecting feedback. Many of these are considered standard skills that are common to most interviewing approaches. In student-driven interviewing, however, they are applied with a distinct eye toward student involvement and solution building. This chapter paves the way for the advanced interviewing skills covered in Chapter 5.

Reflection and Application

1. Pair up with a partner and brainstorm some short responses that practitioners can use to acknowledge and validate moments of silence during interactions with students.

2. Break into groups of three and assign the roles of client, practitioner, and observer. Have the practitioner interview the client about a real or invented problem for about ten minutes, then proceed through the following steps: (a) the observer provides feedback to the practitioner on their nonverbal behaviors; (b) the practitioner provides feedback to the client on their nonverbal behaviors; (c) the practitioner and client discuss the impact that these behaviors had on the conversation and on their perceptions of each other; and (d) everyone discusses the role of nonverbal behavior in interviewing, including special considerations and cautions about interpreting such behavior. Switch roles and repeat.

3. Divide into pairs and designate one person as the client and the other as the practitioner. The practitioner can ask the client questions, or have the client share a story, while offering occasional summaries or paraphrases. Do this for about five minutes and switch roles. After each interview, the client can share feedback on the usefulness of these strategies.

3. Normalizing is a special form of validation. Break into pairs and (a) define normalizing, (b) have one person describe a concern and the other person "normalize" the concern, and (c) switch roles and repeat. After each person has had an opportunity to practice this skill, discuss the benefits of applying this skill in conversations about school behavior problems.

4. This chapter described several ways that practitioners can incorporate playfulness into their conversations with students. Of all these strategies, which ones are most compatible with your style of working with students? Describe a few specific ways that you could incorporate these and other elements of play into your work with young students.

5. During your next meeting with a student, collect outcome and alliance feedback using the ORS and SRS. When the session is finished, make

a few notes on your reaction and the student's reaction to this experience. The ORS and SRS measures can be downloaded free from www.heartandsoulofchange.com.

6. Describe one small step that you are willing to take in your work with students as a result of the information in this chapter.

five

Leading from One Step Behind

II: Advanced Interviewing Skills

Chapter Objectives

- To emphasize the role of language and dialogue in shaping students' perceptions and possibilities;
- To discuss the intentional use of language to promote school solutions;
- To describe and illustrate eight advanced skills in student-driven interviewing.

> Language exerts hidden power, like a moon on the tides.
>
> —Rita Mae Brown

Have you ever been changed by a conversation or viewed a problem much differently after talking with someone about it? The philosophy of social constructionism suggests that we continually construct meanings for ourselves and for the events of our lives in order to make sense of our experience (Gergen, 2009). Although these meanings are unique to the person who forms them, they are shaped and changed through language and social interactions. Social constructionism is discussed in more detail below, followed by the discussion of eight interviewing skills that capitalize on the power of language and dialogue to shape students' perceptions of problems, possibilities, and themselves.

Social Constructionism and the Power of Language

> Truth is not what we discover, but what we create.
>
> —Antoine Saint Exupery

Social constructionism (Gergen, 2009) provides a practical framework for talking with students about problems and solutions. Constructionists believe that a person's sense of what is real and what is possible is constructed rather than discovered:

> The personal meanings and stories that people construct make an important difference to their quality of life experience—for better or worse. Such filters affect the individual's self-concept ... understanding of her past ... and behavior in the future, because we behave in accordance with what we believe to be possible. (Shapiro, Friedberg, & Bardenstein, 2006, pp. 137–138)

The power of language dialogue in shaping self-perceptions has been confirmed by research in the area of social cognition (Fiske & Taylor, 2008). This research suggests that students' conversations with others—whether positive or negative—promote self-perceptions that follow from the conversation. For example, when people were asked to reflect on problems and other negative aspects of their lives, they reported lower levels of self-esteem and happiness than those who reflected on positive aspects (McGuire & McGuire, 1996). These findings suggest that the positive or negative wording of a question may affect not only its answer, but the way students think about themselves and the topic in the future.

Given the power of words and dialogue in shaping perceptions, we need to be mindful of our language when interviewing students. Solution-focused therapists distinguish between problem talk and solution talk (Franklin et al., 2012). Problem talk involves lengthy discussions of the problem, its history, presumed causes, and diagnosis. Solution talk focuses on goals, resources, and possibilities. It is important to provide the opportunity for students to discuss their problems without becoming stuck in problem talk. This chapter provides techniques for increasing solution talk and boosting students' involvement, cooperation, and hope.

Advanced Skills in Student-Driven Interviewing

Each of the following skills involves the intentional use of language to promote solutions. Questioning is discussed first because of its pivotal role in student-driven interviews.

Questioning

> Asking the right question may be the most powerful part of thinking.
>
> —Edward De Bono

Have you ever experienced a question that instantly changed the way you thought about or responded to an important problem or issue in your life? This has happened to me many times, which partly explains my fascination with questions. I have also observed the power of questions with numerous students over the years. As seen with Devon in Chapter 1, one single question can prompt a whole new line of conversation and a different way of viewing and responding to the problem.

Questioning is an essential means of gathering information in all interviewing approaches. In student-driven interviewing, questions serve the additional purpose of promoting change—hence the term "change-focused questions" (Murphy, 2008). Change-focused questions encourage solution talk by focusing on what students deem as important (goals and values) and what they bring to the table that may help them reach their goals (strengths and resources). In discussing the importance of effective questioning, Egan (2010) cautions practitioners about asking too many problem-focused questions:

> Like the rest of us, clients become what they talk about and then go on reinforcing what they have become by talking about it. If you always encourage them to talk about problems, they run the risk of becoming problem people … What clients focus on becomes their chronic reality … So be careful about the questions you ask. They should not keep clients mired in problem talk because problem talk can keep clients immersed in frustration, impotence, and even despair. (p. 292)

The next section describes two types of questions that are commonly used in student-driven interviews: open questions and social relationship questions.

Open Questions

It is important to distinguish between open and closed questions. Open questions broaden the conversation by inviting students to say more about their ideas and perceptions ("What else could you do to make things better at school?"). Closed questions require minimal responses such as "yes" or "no" and are helpful in clarifying certain facts ("Did you pass your math test?; How many days did you attend school last week?"). Closed questions are used sparingly because they put students in the passive role of information providers; they also create an atmosphere of interrogation versus collaboration. Consider how students might respond differently to the following two questions presented in closed and open formats.

- *Question 1 (Closed Format)*: Do you care about your grades in school?
- *Question 1 (Open Format)*: What are your views on the importance of grades in school?
- *Question 2 (Closed Format)*: Now that things are better at school, do you plan to continue these changes?
- *Question 2 (Open Format)*: Now that things are better at school, what are your plans for the future?

As shown above, open questions "open up" conversational pathways and possibilities by inviting students to expand on their ideas and intentions. Here are a few more examples of open questions:

■ How will you know that counseling is working?
■ What can I do to be more helpful?
■ What advice would you give other students who are struggling with this problem?
■ How have you kept things from getting worse?

Even though open questions are favored in student-driven interviewing, closed questions are occasionally used to clarify details. For example, a student who says, "I won't get sent out of class every morning," might be asked a couple of closed questions such as "What is your favorite class?" and "Which class do you get sent out the least from?" If the student gets sent out of science class less than other classes, we could follow up with open questions such as "How are you different in science class?" and "What is different about your science class than your other classes?"

Social Relationship Questions

According to systems theory and social constructionism, school problems are embedded in a social context rather than residing strictly within the student. Students' social interactions and relationships can influence problems and solutions, which is why "social relationship questions" play such an important role in student-driven interviewing. Social relationship questions explore (a) the role and influence of key people, relationships, and social interactions in students' lives, and (b) the social impact of solutions. The following questions fall into the first category:

■ Who do you respect the most in your life? If she were in your shoes, what would she do about this problem? If you called her and told her about this, what would she advise you to do?
■ If I asked your teacher what you could do to improve in class, what would he say?
■ Of all the people you've ever known, who would be most surprised by this problem you're having in school? Why would they be surprised? What do they know about you that others don't?

Here are a few questions that explore the social impact of solutions:

■ Who will be the first people to notice when things start getting better at school? What will they do?
■ How will these school improvements change your relationship with your teachers and parents?
■ What did your teacher do when you turned in your homework yesterday? How was that for you?

Social relationship questions provide useful information while accommodating young people's preference for not being put on the spot by ongoing variations of the tiresome question, "What are you going to do about this problem?" By focusing on the roles and reactions of others, social relationship questions invite students to step outside themselves and consider other perspectives on the problem and potential solutions.

Questioning is a core skill of student-driven interviewing. A well-timed question can be a game changer in the search for school solutions. In my meeting with Devon (Chapter 1), for example, one question shifted the entire focus of the interview from past problems to future solutions. As illustrated throughout this chapter, questions also provide the context for other important skills and techniques.

Complimenting

What flatterers say, try to make true.

—German Proverb

Complimenting students can enhance their motivation and self-efficacy. Compliments are often integrated into questions such as:

- How have you managed to cope with this situation so far?
- Some people would have given up long ago, but not you. Where do you find the strength to keep trying?
- That was a great idea and it worked. How did you come up with it?

These questions yield important information about students' resources while complimenting them on their resilience, success, and ingenuity. Some students have received very few compliments in their lives, which makes it hard for them to muster up the energy and motivation to tackle difficult problems. Compliments acknowledge students' struggles and invite them to adopt a more hopeful view of themselves and their circumstances. For example, asking a student who complains about being stressed out "How have you managed to juggle so many things for so long?" encourages a more hopeful and empowering self-image.

The impact of compliments has also been addressed in research. In a study of the relationship between outcomes and different aspects of solution-focused therapy, the practitioner's use of compliments correlated strongly with positive client outcomes (Linssen & Kerzbeck, 2002). Box 5.1 invites you to reflect on the power of compliments in your life.

The following examples further illustrate how compliments can be woven into interviews with students:

- How have you kept things from getting worse?
- How did you find the courage to tell the truth and apologize?
- What have these improvements taught you about yourself?
- How did you become such a caring person?

Box 5.1 How Do You Respond to Compliments?

Think of a recent compliment you have received in your personal or professional life and consider the following questions: How did you respond to the compliment? How did it affect your motivation and self-confidence?

There are certain compliments I call "formula compliments" because I use them with almost every student I see. Most students, for example, can be complimented for (a) attending the meeting ("Thank you for coming today."), (b) cooperating in the conversation ("I appreciate you answering all my questions."), and (c) trying to improve things at school ("It takes courage to keep trying instead of giving up completely on school."). Even when using formula compliments, it is important to tailor them to the individual student as much as possible ("Evan, your courage to come to these meetings and to keep trying to make things better at school is very impressive, especially with everything else that's going on at home right now.").

Matching the Student's Language

Matching the language of students does not mean trying to sound younger than we are and using the latest student lingo. Most students see right through this and view it as phony. However, echoing certain key words and phrases conveys our acceptance of the student's perspective. The following considerations are helpful in identifying a student's key words and phrases as indicated by italics:

- words and phrases the student uses to describe the problem (I can't seem to *get it together* in that class; I always *get in trouble;* My teachers are *on my case.*)
- frequently used words or phrases (I need to *ace* this exam to pass the class; I need to *chill* more.)
- words and phrases that are unique to the student (I *go into my mind* because it helps me calm down.)
- words that are spoken with additional volume, emphasis, and emotion (He's a *sorry* teacher.).

The following examples illustrate "how to" and "how not to" match the student's language when discussing problems.

Example One: How Not To Match the Student's Language (Antwon, Age 13)

Instead of accepting and matching Antwon's language in the dialogue below, the practitioner tries to talk him into a different way of viewing his teacher. In addition to invalidating Antwon's perspective and jeopardizing the alliance, the practitioner demonstrates another barrier to effective interviewing—the use of professional jargon.

School Practitioner (SP):   Why do you think Mr. Young (history teacher) referred you to me?

Antwon: He's a jerk, that's why. He gets on me all the time. He has it out for me. He lectures about stupid stuff and then wonders why we mess around in class. Nobody likes him. He gets on people a lot. He can't teach, so he yells at us instead. He ought to refer himself for counseling. I'm tired of him getting on me about everything.

SP: That's pretty harsh, isn't it? [Challenging Antwon's perception of his teacher.]

Antwon: What do you mean?

SP: Well, maybe Mr. Young is a conscientious teacher and a disciplinarian who runs a structured classroom. [Using professional jargon.]

Antwon: What?

SP: It sounds like you and Mr. Young have a personality conflict and communication issues. [More jargon.]

Antwon: If you say so. [Antwon shrugs his shoulders, scoots a little lower in the chair, and starts making plans for the weekend.]

Example Two: How To Match the Student's Language (Antwon Revisited)

Observe the differences between the previous exchange and the following one in which the practitioner accepts and matches Antwon's language (key words and phrases are italicized).

SP: Why do you think Mr. Young referred you to me?

Antwon: He's a jerk, that's why. He *gets on me* all the time. He has it out for me. He lectures about stupid stuff and then he wonders why we mess around in class. Nobody likes him. He *gets on people* a lot. He can't teach, so he yells at us instead. He ought to refer himself for counseling. I'm tired of him *getting on me* about everything.

SP: How does he get on you? [Reflecting a key phrase in Antwon's comments.]

Antwon: He's always asking me questions that he knows I won't be able to answer. He sends me out of class to the principal's office for little stuff. Some students mess around as much as I do and they never get sent out.

SP: How else does he get on you? [Using an open question to encourage elaboration.]

Antwon: He says rude stuff about me in front of the whole class. Instead of talking to me in the hallway, he says it in front of everybody. I hate that.

SP: That must be frustrating for you.

Antwon: It is. ["Staying with" Antwon's perception of his teacher; Antwon responds in kind by staying with the conversation instead of checking out and shutting down.]

Matching Antwon's language helped to set a cooperative tone and encouraged him to share more details about his perceptions and experiences in history class. Matching the language of students enhances the alliance by letting them know that we are listening to them and taking them seriously—something that young people greatly appreciate from helpers and other adults.

Using the Language of Curiosity

Never lose a holy curiosity.

—Albert Einstein

Adopting a position of curiosity helps us to approach students' from a fresh perspective that honors their perceptions, goals, and resources. Curiosity conveys our openness to new ideas and willingness to learn from students. Leading from one step behind requires us to be "curious and tentative" rather than "absolute and certain" (Murphy, 2008), and to lead by invitation rather than imposition (see Box 5.2).

Put yourself in the student's shoes as you read the following scenarios in which two practitioners—Dr. Smart and Dr. Curious—introduce Charlene (age 11) to a different view of her teachers. Pay close attention to the practitioner's language in each scenario.

Dr. Smart, the Certain and Impositional Practitioner: When we met last week, Charlene, you were saying that your teachers were too strict and they didn't care about you. I've thought about that, along with some other things we discussed, and I think you've got your teachers all wrong [statement of certainty]. They actually care a lot about you. It is because they care about you that they take the time and effort to make sure you do your homework and get good grades. ["It is because ..." implies absolute truth] You need to start thinking differently [statement of imposition].

Dr. Curious, the Tentative and Invitational Practitioner: When we met last week, Charlene, you were saying that your teachers were too strict and they didn't care about you. *I'm wondering* if there could be any other *possible*

Box 5.2 Invitation versus Imposition

Few things shut down a conversation and relationship faster than one person trying to force ideas onto another—something that happens a lot between adults and young people. Regardless of how good our intentions or ideas are, students have to decide for themselves whether or not to accept them. Instead of imposing our opinions on students by telling them how they should think or act, we can offer ideas in a tentative and invitational manner that allows students to freely accept or reject them. The invitational approach is not only more respectful to students; it also increases their involvement, ownership, and accountability in the change process.

explanations for what your teachers are doing [statement of curiosity]. *I'm not sure* if this is on target [tentative statement], but you're the best judge of that so I'll tell you what I was thinking and let you decide. *Could it be that* one of the reasons your teachers get on you about turning in homework and getting good grades is because they *might* actually care about you enough to remind you to turn it in so you can get better grades? *I don't know*, what do you think? [statement of invitation]

The quickest way to ruin a good idea is to force it on students against their will, as Dr. Smart did in the first scenario. Dr. Curious offered the same ideas in a more collaborative way that invited Carlene to decide for herself. Dr. Smart led by imposition; Dr. Curious, by invitation. Who do you think the student would be more willing to cooperate with?

In addition to inviting students to freely accept or reject our ideas, the language of curiosity preserves our credibility and flexibility when our ideas are viewed as inaccurate or unhelpful. When a student rejects an idea that is presented as a possibility rather than a fact, we can simply move on instead defending or justifying it. Presenting our opinions and interpretations as if they were facts boxes us and students into a corner, whereas the following phrases preserve our flexibility and invite students to choose for themselves:

- Could it be that …?
- I'm not sure if this makes sense, but …
- I'm wondering …
- Suppose you tried … What do you think might happen then?
- Is it possible that …?
- What do you think about that?

Using the Language of Empowerment

The concept of empowerment is captured in the popular serenity prayer: "Grant me the serenity to accept the things I cannot change, the courage to change the things I can, and the wisdom to know the difference." The language of empowerment helps students to distinguish between the changeable and unchangeable aspects of the school situation, and to focus on *their* role in changing what they can in school.

When students are asked about problems or about what needs to happen to improve things at school, they sometimes refer to what *others* need to do differently:

- Maybe I would get better grades if my parents would stop nagging me so much.
- My teacher doesn't like me so why should I even try?
- Everything would be fine if I had a different teacher.

These comments fix students' attention on people and circumstances over which they have little control. As illustrated with Miranda, age 15, we can validate students' frustrations while exploring what they can do to improve things at school.

School Practitioner (SP):	You know this situation better than I do, so I wanted to ask you what needs to happen differently at school to make things better for you.
Miranda:	Fire the teachers.
SP:	Fire the teachers? [Mirroring Miranda's words.]
Miranda:	They just sit at their desks and drink coffee and read the paper and give a bunch of tests. They don't know what they're doing and they don't really teach you anything.
SP:	That sounds frustrating. [Validating Miranda's perceptions.]
Miranda:	It is.
SP:	How does that make things worse for you at school when you feel this way about your teachers? [Shifting the focus from the teachers to Miranda.]
Miranda:	I don't care. If they're not going to teach me anything, why should I care?
SP:	That's a good question. Why should you care?
Miranda:	(Shrugs shoulders.)
SP:	Do you care?
Miranda:	No. Well, kind of.
SP:	Kind of?
Miranda:	I want to do okay so I don't end up like my cousin. She flunked out of high school and she can't even get a job.
SP:	And you want something different for yourself?
Miranda:	Yes.

[A few minutes later in the conversation, the school practitioner and Miranda explore what she is willing to do to change things at school.]

SP:	I'm not sure how easy it's going to be to change things at school. It seems like it's going to take some hard work.
Miranda:	I don't know. Maybe.
SP:	Well, I'm just thinking that your teachers are going to be the same, and I'm wondering what you can do to get closer to your goal of doing okay in school regardless of what your teachers do or how they act. Because they're probably going to do things that you don't like. How are you going to resist letting your teachers take you off course of your goal to do a better in school and not end up like your cousin?

The remainder of the interview focused on Miranda's actions and plans instead of the attitudes and actions of her teachers.

The following questions invite students to focus on their role in building solutions:

- Imagine that your parents suddenly stopped nagging you. What would you do differently if that happened? What is blocking you from doing that now?
- How have you managed to cope with this so far? How could those strategies help you improve things at school?
- What have you learned about yourself through all this? How can you use that information to reach your goals?
- What will be the first small sign that things are getting just a little bit better at school? What can you do to make that happen?

Some students experience disempowering circumstances on a regular basis—child abuse, unstable home environments, and unsafe neighborhoods are a few such examples. The language of empowerment does not deny these harsh realities, but respectfully invites students to focus on their goals, resources, and natural desire for growth and self-sufficiency.

Using the Language of Qualification

Ongoing problems can wear students down and create a negative and hopeless outlook. As a result, students may describe problems in all-or-none terms as illustrated in the following statements:

- I've *never* done well in school.
- The teacher *always* gets on my case.
- My mom and I fight *constantly*.

In responding to these statements, we can use the language of qualification to invite a more flexible view without discounting students' comments. The following examples illustrate the practitioner's use of qualifying phrases (in italics).

Example One

Student: My social studies teacher (Mr. Thomas) hates me now. It seems like everything I do is wrong. He yells at me constantly in class.

School Practitioner: So you and Mr. Thomas clash *a lot of the time* these days and *don't get along very well.*

Example Two

Student: I never pay attention in class anymore.

School Practitioner: Okay. So you've had *a lot of* trouble paying attention in class *so far* this year, right?

The practitioner's use of qualification invites a more hopeful view that allows for the possibility of change without challenging or discounting the student's perspective. Like other strategies in this chapter, qualification can be embedded in questions and comments to students.

Using the Language of Presupposition

And what before is left behind, that which was not comes to be, and every
minute gives place to another.

—Ovid, The Metamorphoses

A presupposition is a statement or question that implies something without coming out and saying it directly. Presupposition is a classic technique of lawyers who
try to sway the jury's view of a witness by asking questions such as "Do you still
cheat on your tax returns?" Regardless of the answer, the question implies that the
witness has cheated on previous tax returns. This technique can be used in a more
positive way with students.

In student-driven interviewing, presupposition is used to encourage hope by
inviting students to focus on their strengths, successes, and possibilities (MacMartin, 2008). Instead of asking "Have you ever done well in school?" we could ask
"When have you done a little better in school?" The italicized words in the following questions are used to instill hope by implying that positive change is not only
possible, but inevitable:

- How *will* you be able to tell *when* things start getting better in history
  class?
- What *will* be the first small sign that things are improving at school?
- Who *will* be the first to notice and what *will* they do?
- How *will* your teachers and parents treat you differently *when* things
  change at school?

As illustrated above, the presupposition or "inevitability" of change is conveyed by
future-focused words such as "will" and "when." The language of presupposition
enhances outcomes by (a) inviting students to focus on future possibilities and
(b) conveying our faith in their ability to improve their lives.

Using Sentence Completion Strategies

In sentence completion strategies, practitioners provide the first part of a sentence
and students finish it in their own words. Here are some examples:

- When I have a problem, it helps to …
- I want to be the kind of person who …
- The person in my life who helps me the most is …
- The worst part about school is …
- The best part about school is …

Sentence completion is a flexible strategy that can be tailored to fit any topic or
student. This strategy helps to hold students' attention during the conversation by
mixing up the format and providing a different way to gather information. The
following example illustrates the use of sentence completion in a brief exchange
with Tyrone, a 5-year-old student referred for hyperactivity and excessive talking
in class.

School Practitioner (SP): Is it okay if I ask you some questions about school?
Tyrone: Yes.
SP: Thank you. I know this game where I say something and then you finish it. How does that sound?
Tyrone: Okay.
SP: Great. So here we go. The thing I like best about school is ...
Tyrone: My friends.
SP: The best thing about my friends is ...
Tyrone: They're nice.
SP: Good job. You want to keep going?
Tyrone: Yes.

[Later in the conversation]

SP: When I get in trouble at school, it helps me when ...
Tyrone: I lay down.
SP: What else helps you calm down in school, Tyrone?

Many students, especially younger ones like Tyrone, are not used to having lengthy discussions with adults. Sentence completion makes it easier on students by giving them a running start in responding to our questions. This and other advanced skills in student-driven interviewing are briefly described and illustrated in Table 5.1.

Summary and Conclusions

The philosophy of social constructionism proposes that language and dialogue play a large role in the way that students perceive and respond to school behavior problems. This chapter describes eight skills that use language in change-focused ways such as questioning, complimenting, and matching the student's language. Using the language of curiosity, empowerment, qualification, and presupposition facilitates solutions by putting students in the driver's seat and bolstering their hope. Sentence completion strategies provide another way to mix up the interviewing format and engage students in solution building. The skills in Chapters 4 and 5 are woven into the specific strategies of student-driven interviewing, which are covered next.

Reflection and Application

1. Provide an example of solution talk and problem talk in interviewing students. What are the advantages of encouraging solution talk in conversations with students referred for school behavior problems?
2. Describe the difference between open and closed questions and provide an example of each. Why are open-ended questions used more often in student-driven interviews?

TABLE 5.1 Advanced Skills of Student-Driven Interviewing

Skill	Description	Example
Questioning	A means of gathering information and encouraging new ways of viewing and responding to problems; promotes change by increasing solution talk	"What do you think you could do to improve your relationship with your teacher?" (open question); "Who do you admire most, and what would this person advise you to do about this problem?" (social relationship question)
Complimenting	Commenting positively on students' attributes and actions in ways that enhance their confidence, hope, and motivation; can be integrated into questions	"I'm impressed with your courage to keep coming to school and trying to make things better. What has kept you from giving up?"
Matching the student's language	Echoing certain key words and phrases that the student uses to describe the problem	Student: "My teacher is always getting on my case." Practitioner: "How does your teacher get on your case?"; "What have you found helpful in keeping your teacher off your case?"
Using the language of curiosity	Presenting ideas in curious and tentative (vs. absolute and certain) ways	Beginning certain statements or suggestions with, "I wonder if . . .," "I'm not sure, but . . .," and "Could it be that . . ."
Using the language of empowerment	Using questions and comments that acknowledge students' influence on school problems and solutions	Student: "I would do better if my teachers would just back off." Practitioner: "How willing are you to try something different to get your teachers to back off?"
Using the language of qualification	Responding to students' all-or-none language with qualifying words or phrases that convey a more flexible and hopeful view	Student: "My teacher and I never get along." Practitioner: "So you and your teacher have had a lot of rough spots lately?"
Using the language of presupposition	A statement or question that implies or "presupposes" something without directly stating it; instills hope by inviting students to imagine a better future	Asking, "How will your teachers treat you differently when things start getting a little better at school?"
Using sentence completion strategies	Providing the first part of a sentence and asking students to finish it; a playful way to increase students' involvement while learning about them and their perspectives	"My biggest concern about school is . . ." "The best part about school is . . ." "I want to be the kind of person who . . ."

3. Provide two examples of social relationship questions that you could use with students.

4. Why are compliments important in working with students who are referred for school behavior problems? List two compliments that you could use with such students.

5. The next time you're with someone who is nagging or complaining about something, stay quiet and listen without commenting for a while. After a while, when there is a gap in the complaining, give them a sincere compliment about something you heard in their comments. It is important that the compliment is anchored in something they said.

6. Break into pairs and assume the roles of client and practitioner. Have the client share a concern, after which the practitioner can use the language of curiosity to explore different views of the problem. Switch roles and repeat the exercise.

7. Describe one small step that you are willing to take in your work with students as a result of the information in this chapter.

part three
Strategies

six

Setting the Stage for Student Involvement and Solutions

Chapter Objectives

- To emphasize the importance of first impressions;
- To describe methods for arranging the physical environment in ways that promote students' engagement and cooperation;
- To present strategies for orienting students to the helping process;
- To discuss the role of hope in setting the stage for student involvement and solutions.

> The beginning is the most important part of any work.
>
> —Plato

One of the major advantages of solution-focused brief therapy is its efficiency (de Shazer et al., 2007). However, the term "brief" does not mean being pushy and rushing people into solutions. Efficiency results from recruiting students' strengths and resources right away instead of conducting time-consuming diagnostic assessments.

In schools and other agencies, intervention services are usually initiated through the completion of intake or referral forms. These forms typically request information about the problem with little or no emphasis on clients' goals and resources. Referral forms often represent the first step in the school-based intervention process, so it is important that schools create forms that focus on goals and solutions as well as problems.

You may not have control over the procedures and forms that are used in your setting, but you do have control over your words and actions during the first few moments of contact with students. Following a discussion of first impressions, this chapter provides practical strategies that set the stage for student involvement and solutions during the opening moments of conversation.

Making Positive First Impressions

I remember my parents saying "make a good first impression" as I left the house to interview for a newspaper delivery job at age 10. That was good advice for a child on a vocational mission (I got the job), and it is good advice for school practitioners meeting with students for the first time. Research in social psychology indicates that people's first impression of a person influences their subsequent judgments about the person's attractiveness and competence (Ambady & Skowronski, 2008). First impressions are created quickly (Willis & Todorov, 2006). Once created, they are not easily changed. The influence and staying power of first impressions has been demonstrated with children as young as 5 years old (Johnson et al., 2000). The fact that first impressions exert a powerful influence long after they are created is referred to as the "primacy effect."

The primacy effect suggests that positive initial interactions with students predispose them to favorable impressions of us and our services; negative first impressions predispose them to unfavorable perceptions. Positive first impressions enhance the likelihood of successful outcomes while negative impressions lead students to drop out of the helping process, psychologically and literally (Dennis et al., 2004; Miller et al., 2006; Zuroff & Blatt, 2006).

Arranging the Physical Setting

The setting in which we meet students can affect their impression of us. The physical environment is less important than the conversation itself, but it is worth some attention. While we may not have full control over the places in which we meet students, we should try to arrange the setting in ways that convey respect and promote the student's comfort and cooperation. It is important for practitioners to be comfortable as well, but not at the expense of the student. For example, a practitioner who likes glitzy furniture and flashy wall hangings might want to tone it down a bit if students seem uncomfortable or distracted in this environment. Given the diversity of students and circumstances that you may encounter on a daily basis, the following guidelines are offered as general considerations that will vary based on the particulars of the student and situation. Many of the guidelines and strategies are not research-validated—instead, they are based on my own experience and on the overall goals of student-driven interviewing.

Simplify

I have never had a student complain about an office or meeting room being too bland or simple, including rooms with little more than two chairs and a table.

Students are not there to evaluate our sense of fashion and interior design. Offices that are full of tantalizing sights and objects can be very distracting for young children who like to touch and examine every interesting object they see. In deciding what to include in the room, it is useful to view it from the student's perspective. This may involve entering the room, sitting in the chair that students use, and imagining how they might respond to the setting. You can also ask students and colleagues to visit your office and offer ideas for making it as inviting and comfortable as possible.

Use Respectful Seating Arrangements

While most helping professionals are trained to move out from behind the desk in working with clients, I have observed less attention to this guideline among those who work with young people. It is especially important, however, to attend to displays of status and power when working with young people. When students enter into a counseling relationship with an adult, they may automatically assume a passive role and expect to be told what to do. Seating arrangements may subtly reinforce this assumption and work against students' involvement in the conversation. Consider the situation in which the practitioner sits in a large, overstuffed chair behind a big desk while the student sits in a plain chair across the office. Seating arrangements that blatantly portray the practitioner as "the leader" and the student as "the follower" are antithetical to the goal of involving students as essential partners in solution building.

The following strategies promote a collaborative atmosphere that conveys respect for students and enhances their participation; some strategies will be more feasible than others, and some will need to be adjusted to fit the student and physical environment.

- Maintain a clear line of vision between you and the student, and reduce any barriers such as plants, telephones, or books.
- Position yourself at or below the student's eye level when possible—sit in the same size chair as the student, let the student take the big chair and you take the small one, or sit on the floor with the student.
- Conduct the conversation while taking a walk, tossing a ball, playing a board game, or eating lunch with the student.
- All of these strategies demonstrate our willingness to structure the physical environment to the comfort and preferences of students.

Beginning the Conversation

It is the nature of beginning that something new is started which cannot be expected from whatever may have happened before.

—Hannah Arendt

When we meet with students for the first time, we usually know more about them than they know about us—which places us in a dominant position before the conversation even begins. It is crucial, therefore, that we begin the interview in a hopeful and respectful way. The following sections describe strategies for doing so.

Introductions and Icebreakers

It is important to choose words carefully when working with young people because they are very alert to what we say and how we say it—especially when we first meet them. Many students have never experienced a counseling relationship and are understandably suspicious or angry about having to participate. Sometimes students are not even told why they were referred. These issues, coupled with the fact that most students have never met us prior to the first session, suggest that we approach them in ways that are as comfortable and nonthreatening as possible. One way to do this is to ask questions that convey respect for their preferences, perceptions, and resources.

After introducing myself, I ask students how they would like to be addressed. Many referral forms state the student's formal name, such as Thomas, though the student may be more comfortable with Tom. I let them choose which chair to sit in and ask if the seating arrangement is agreeable to them. These opening moves may seem mundane and obvious, but they express our willingness to honor the student's preferences from the very outset of the relationship.

Once we are settled, I might ask about a hobby or interest listed on the referral form. Questions about recent community events or how long they have lived in the neighborhood are also useful icebreakers that help students to ease into the conversation. These short exchanges may reveal students' strengths, interests, or other resources that can be applied toward solutions. Listening closely to what students say during the opening moments of the interview helps to clarify their overall frame of reference and communication style.

I always ask students for their permission to take notes during the session to help me remember what we discuss. I explain that they are free to look at my notes anytime during the session and to photocopy them at the end of the meeting. This type of transparency strengthens trust and reduces any mystery about the content and purpose of the notes.

In addition to starting the first session with some nonthreatening questions and small talk, I may request students' help with a simple task as illustrated below:

- Could you help me move this chair out of the way?
- Would you grab one side of this table so we can move it?
- I need to hang this picture on the wall and it's hard for me to judge whether it's hanging straight. Can you help me with this?

These requests provide safe opportunities for students to be successful on their very first task in the relationship, which helps them to ease into the conversation and with positive momentum.

Rodney, Age 10

Rodney was referred for services by his teachers due to disruptive classroom behavior. As I entered the school to meet with Rodney, the principal ushered me into a small storage room for art supplies. (I've been in much worse.) I was moving art supplies from a table when Rodney arrived. I asked him to give me a hand and commented that he probably wasn't expecting to do physical labor. Rodney smiled and helped me clear the table and set up a couple chairs.

I asked for Rodney's permission to videotape the meeting and for his help in setting up the tripod and camera. I fumbled a bit with the camera because it was different from the one I typically used. Rodney looked at the camera for a few seconds and proceeded to attach it to the tripod as I assisted. When I asked how he figured it out so quickly, Rodney said that he was always good at putting things together. I also asked what else he was good at and enjoyed doing outside of school. We discussed music and other interests for a few minutes, and Rodney was cooperative throughout the remainder of the session. Helping me with the table and camera allowed Rodney to ease into the relationship in a way that was more comfortable than jumping right in with a lot of questions about school.

In selecting physical tasks to use as icebreakers, remember to pick a task that you could genuinely use help with—no matter how small it is. As you incorporate this strategy into your own work, you will discover other tasks that can be used to help students ease into the conversation in ways that are safe and comfortable for them.

Orienting Students to the Helping Process

After a couple of minutes of small talk we can ask students if they know why they are meeting with us. When students receive minimal information about why they were referred for services, it is important to explain the reasons for the referral as clearly as possible. Consider the following exchange with Rosario, age 8, referred by her teacher (Ms. Jones) due to concerns about her grades and attention skills.

School Practitioner (SP):	Do you know why you're meeting with me today?
Rosario:	(Shrugs shoulders to indicate "I don't know.")
SP:	Did Ms. Jones talk to you about meeting with me?
Rosario:	Kind of.
SP:	What did she say?
Rosario:	She said you talk to kids about being better in school.
SP:	That's right. Ms. Jones wants you to pay attention in class so you can learn a lot in school, and she wanted me to talk with you to help you. Does that make sense?
Rosario:	Yes.
SP:	Do you want to ask me anything else about why Ms. Jones wanted us to meet?
Rosario:	No.

Ensuring that students understand why they were referred lays an initial foundation for a trusting and productive working relationship. Once students know why they are there, we can describe our approach to helping them. Prefatory comments, as they are called in the literature, include statements about the practitioner's overall approach to intervention, the rationale for the approach, and the general manner in which the helping process will work. I recommend simple, jargon-free language as illustrated in the following comments to a 12-year-old student referred for individual counseling:

> I want to tell you how this works. I need you to teach me what you want school to be like and what I can do to help. You know yourself better than anybody, so I'll need to ask you some questions about what you want and what might help make things better for you at school. We might come up with some ideas right away, or it might take us a while. I'll never try to force you to do something you don't want to do or talk about something you don't want to talk about. I don't like people doing that with me, so I won't do it with you. I'll also check with you to see how things are working. The only way I'll know if I'm helping you is to ask you, so I'll need your help on that, okay? Do you have any questions?

Explaining the helping process enhances outcomes by preparing students for what lies ahead, increasing their expectancy of change (Costantino & DeGeorge, 2008), and strengthening the therapeutic alliance (Shirk, Karver, & Brown, 2011). Prefatory statements lay the foundation for cooperation by sending the message that *we work for the student, not the other way around.* This message of respect and collaboration is continued in the sections that follow.

Viewing Students as Capable

> The way you see people is the way you treat them, and the way you treat them is what they become.
>
> —Goethe

Our initial words and actions send strong messages about how we view students and their role in building solutions. First impressions are quickly formed and slowly changed, so we should carefully consider our opening moves. It all starts with attitude. Our attitude toward students affects everything we do in the helping process. Research on the self-fulfilling prophecy suggests that we usually see what we are looking for in others. As illustrated with Raymond in Chapter 1, the phrase "seeing is believing" might be more accurately stated as "believing is seeing." Based on the practical notion that some views are more useful than others when it comes to helping people change, I encourage you to view students as vital contributors to solutions from the opening moments of contact with them.

Promoting Hope

> Hope is necessary in every condition.
>
> —Samuel Johnson

The powerful role of hope and expectancy has been discussed throughout the history of the helping professions (Costantino, Glass, Arnkoff, Ametrano, & Smith, 2011). Dating back to the early 1900s, Alfred Adler emphasized the importance of encouragement and hope in therapeutic relationships (Mozak & Maniacci, 2008). He believed that hope was enhanced primarily through the practitioner's expression of faith in the client. Adler's emphasis on the importance of hope is every bit as relevant today as it was a century ago. There are two types of hope that impact outcomes—the student's hope and the practitioner's hope.

The Student's Hope

It is not surprising that students may enter services feeling defeated and demoralized given that (a) the problem may have persisted for weeks or months, (b) several interventions may have been implemented without success, (c) they see the situation as out of their control, and (d) they enter services at someone else's request. Research findings link outcomes to clients' expectancy of change (Whalley et al., 2008) and confidence in their ability to contribute to solutions (Gassman & Grawe, 2006). We can enhance outcomes by treating students in empowering ways that boost hope and counteract "problem fatigue." Costantino et al. (2011) strongly recommend that practitioners integrate hope-promoting strategies into the change process, noting that the power of client expectancy has been undervalued despite a large body of research linking it to successful outcomes.

In traditional clinical practice, the initial interview is aimed primarily at diagnosing people and their problems. These interviews are heavy in problem talk about deficiencies, weaknesses, and other aspects of what's wrong with clients. Most of the students I meet are well aware of their problems and deficiencies, so it is not surprising that they are more responsive to conversations that emphasize strengths and resources over pathology and deficits. I learned this the hard way during my first year of practice when a high school student named Roger taught me an unforgettable lesson about the importance of beginning the first interview on a hopeful and encouraging note. Box 6.1 describes my experience with Roger.

Box 6.1 Roger's R-Rated Lesson, OR How "Not To" Promote Hope in the First Session

Like many initial interviews, my first session with Roger began with a series of diagnostic questions aimed at clarifying and analyzing the problem—noncompliance and talking out and class. About 15 minutes into the meeting, Roger stood up and bolted from my office—but not before sharing his expletive-laced opinion of our conversation. Embedded in Roger's spirited feedback was a clear message that went something like this: "The last thing I need from you is another reminder of how screwed up I am." As a rookie practitioner with a strong desire to be seen as competent, my first reaction was to blame Roger's outburst on his irrational anger or resistance to treatment. I told myself, "It couldn't have been anything I did, right?" Wrong!

Fortunately, my ego-protective first reaction was replaced by a more reasonable explanation when I considered the situation from Roger's standpoint. Roger's perspective was further clarified when I apologized later that day, at which point we regrouped and started over. Roger said, "I know I've got problems. My family does, too. But why do I always have to talk about that crap with everyone?" Why indeed?

Roger taught me exactly what the outcome research indicates: A deliberate effort to empower people's hope and resources from the opening moments of interaction promotes cooperation and solutions. By the way, Roger apologized for his language and behavior in our first meeting. I thanked him for the apology … and the lesson!

Although clients' hope has received most of the attention in the research literature, our hope as practitioners also contributes to successful outcomes as described next.

The Practitioner's Hope

Our success as practitioners is influenced by our belief in people's ability to change and in the helping process itself (Wampold, 2010). Our hope is based largely on how we view students, and our view of students is a matter of choice, not fact. We can view students from a diagnostic perspective, which tends to diminish hope. Or we can see them as temporarily stuck yet capable of changing—a view that is more likely to boost our expectations about students and intervention services.

Maintaining one's optimism in the midst of serious problems is easier said than done; it's hard to "keep the fire burning" when you spend the majority of your professional life addressing serious problems. Referrals and school files typically include extensive details and reports about the student's problems with little or no attention to strengths and resources. The mere act of reading a referral and school file can lead to a pessimistic attitude before we ever lay eyes on the student. Student-driven interviewing counteracts problem overload and replaces it with a more hopeful perspective.

In addition to improving outcomes, a hopeful attitude buffers us against professional burnout. Practitioners who focus on clients' deficits and dysfunction appear to be more prone to burnout and less effective than practitioners who focus on strengths and are more hopeful about their clients (Gassman & Grawe, 2006; Snyder, Michael, & Cheavens, 1999). Hopeful practitioners develop a knack for seeing valuable qualities in students that they don't see in themselves; in doing so, they are modeling the same attitude toward students that they would like students to have toward themselves—an attitude of optimism and possibility.

The methods in this chapter help practitioners begin the conversation in hopeful ways even in the most serious circumstances. This hope is not based on a naïve view of the problem, the pain, or the hard work involved in making changes.

Instead, it emerges from an abiding trust in students' resilience and resources—and in the helping process itself.

Summary and Conclusions

This chapter describes strategies that set the stage for students' involvement in solution building by inviting their input, resources, and hope from the very first moments of contact. Icebreakers and prefatory comments orient students to the helping process and allow them to ease into the relationship at their own pace and in their own way. Recognizing students' opinions and resources encourages them to view themselves in more hopeful, empowering ways. The emphasis on collaboration, resources, and hope begins when we first meet students and continues throughout the helping process.

Reflection and Application

1. Create two items on a "Referral for Services" form that would help to identify students' strengths and resources.
2. Why are first impressions important to consider during initial contacts with students? Describe two actions that you can take to enhance students' first impressions of you.
3. The physical setting in which you meet with students should complement your overall approach to the extent possible. How could you arrange and use your setting in ways that complement your approach and boost your effectiveness with students?
4. In pairs or small groups, brainstorm a list of icebreaker tasks that you could ask students to help with when you first meet with them.
5. Prefatory or "orienting" comments improve counseling outcomes. Write out a short set of prefatory comments that you could use to introduce students to your approach. Pair up with a partner and practice presenting your comments.
6. Hope plays a prominent role in setting the stage for solutions to school behavior problems—hope on the part of both students and practitioners. Describe two strategies for promoting hope in students along with two strategies for maintaining your own hope as a school practitioner.
7. Describe one small step that you are willing to take in your work with students as a result of the information in this chapter.

seven

Discussing Problems in Solution-Focused Ways

If we spoke a different language, we would perceive a somewhat different world.

—Ludwig Wittgenstein

Chapter Objectives

- To present strategies for acknowledging and prioritizing students' concerns;
- To illustrate techniques for helping students describe changeable problems;
- To provide strategies for exploring environmental factors, problem impact, and solution attempts;
- To discuss techniques for clarifying students' perceptions of problems and solutions.

I met Nick several years ago when he was referred by his third-grade teachers for disruptive classroom behavior and peer problems. When I asked him what he wanted to change at school, Nick mentioned several complaints about his teachers and classmates, about the way the school was run, and about being assigned to after-school detention almost every day. I listened for a few minutes and then asked if there was anything about school that he liked. He stopped for a couple of seconds, looked at me, and picked up right where he left off with the complaints. Nick was not finished being heard when I interrupted him with my question. I took the hint and stayed out of his way as he shared additional details of his perspective on the problem.

Rushing Nick into solution talk against his will would have been a big mistake. Hearing and validating students' experiences is a key step in changing behavior problems. In the beginning of our work with students, this often involves discussing the problem and related factors. These discussions allow students to describe the problem from their perspective, which serves to clarify their ideas about the problem and solution. Understanding students' struggles and perceptions helps us validate their experience and tailor services to their unique preferences and perspectives—all of which contribute to an effective relationship. In other words, it is possible to discuss problems in ways that enhance solutions.

Acknowledging and Prioritizing Students' Concerns

If you want others to be happy, practice compassion.

— The Dalai Lama

Behavior problems rarely come in neat little packages. Most referrals involve social, behavioral, and academic components. It is important to acknowledge all concerns while exploring the ones that are most pressing from the student's perspective. The following questions help students prioritize their concerns:

- Of all these concerns, which one is most important to you?
- There is a lot going on here. What do you want to work on first?
- If you could change one of these problems instantly, which one would it be? Why that one?
- [Pointing to the student's completed Outcome Rating Scale] Which of these areas is most important to you?
- If we could change just one of the things you mentioned, which one would make the biggest difference in your school life?

Consider the following conversation with Brandon, an 11-year-old student who mentioned several concerns about school.

School Practitioner (SP):	So, you get in trouble for talking in class, arguing with other students, and not turning in homework. Which of these do you want to work on first?
Brandon:	I guess the homework.
SP:	Okay. Why is the homework important to you?
Brandon:	My mom always bugs me and asks about it. So does my teacher.
SP:	So you're getting it at school and home.
Brandon:	Yes.
SP:	How do they bug you about it?
Brandon:	My mom is always asking me if I did my homework and things like that. Every night it's, "What

	do you have for homework? You better do your homework."
SP:	So when things get better with homework, your life will be better at home and school because your mom and teacher won't bug you as much about it. Is that it?
Brandon:	Yes.
SP:	Interesting. I can see why you want to work on the homework first.

Helping students prioritize problems helps to boost their hope by narrowing a wide range of problems into a specific and manageable focus. As evidenced with Brandon, future-focused words such as "when" and "will" also can be folded into questions to enhance students' hope and motivation ("Brandon, are you saying that *when* things get better with homework, your life *will* be better at home and school?").

Efficiency is always important, but we should never rush students at the expense of the alliance. Most students have struggled with the problem for weeks or months before they meet with us. Providing ample time for students to describe their concerns and frustrations assures them that they have been heard and gives us a better understanding of their experience.

In teaching classes and workshops, I am often asked what to do when students want to work on something that seems trivial or unimportant to the practitioner. First, I have found that students often identify concerns that are very similar to those of their teachers and parents. Second, our ideas about the significance of a problem are just that—*our* ideas based on *our* perspective. What students view as important may or may not seem important to their teachers, parents, or service providers. Even when that occurs, it still may be best to address the student's concern first because their involvement is essential to the success of any school-based intervention. When students are permitted to work on their most pressing concerns, they may become more receptive to working on other issues.

Describing Changeable Problems

Sometimes the situation is only a problem because it is looked at in a certain way.

—Edward de Bono

Once we help students prioritize their concerns, we can determine exactly what a particular concern or problem looks like. For example, if students say that they have a "bad attitude," we need to find out what that means from their perspective. Everyday language is full of abstract words that mean different things to different people—immature, disrespectful, spacey, antsy, unmotivated, aggressive, ADHD, and so forth. The only way to determine what these words mean to a person is to obtain specific descriptions.

Consider the example of Chancey, a 16-year-old student who said that her biggest problem was "being disorganized." When I asked what she did or did not do that reflected disorganization, she was able to describe several changeable behaviors that she wanted to work on—spending less time on the phone, making a "to do" list each morning, and cleaning her room once a week. Chancey became more energized as the conversation shifted from the unchangeable trait of disorganization to the description of specific, changeable actions.

The language used to describe Chancey's problem facilitated a solution. Action descriptions ("hitting and cursing") are always preferable to diagnostic labels and other abstract terms ("aggression") when it comes to discussing and resolving problems. O'Hanlon and Bertolino (2002) similarly recommend using "videotalk," which refers to describing a problem exactly as it would look on a videotape while refraining from interpretations and diagnostic labels. The encouragement of videotalk is particularly useful when students describe problems in vague or interpretive terms such as "hyper" or "bad attitude." A more changeable problem will result from asking students to describe it as if they were watching it on video. Consider the following videotalk descriptions of a student's bad attitude: "I'm late for classes, I don't do a lot of homework, and I talk to my friends during class." Each of these behaviors is easier to see and change than the student's "bad attitude."

When students use vague terms to describe the problem, the following questions can be used to elicit action descriptions and videotalk:

- If I videotaped this problem, what would I see and hear?
- If we were watching a movie of this problem, what would we see first? Then what?
- What would I see if I was a fly on the classroom wall?
- I want to make sure I have a clear picture of what is happening. Can you describe a recent example of the problem?

Helping students describe changeable problems is illustrated below with Kevin, a 9-year-old student who was diagnosed with Attention-Deficit Hyperactivity Disorder (ADHD).

School Practitioner (SP):	Do you know why your parents wanted you to meet with me?
Kevin:	Because I'm ADHD and I get real hyper, especially at school.
SP:	What would I see if I watched you being hyper in school?
Kevin:	I'd be moving around in my seat and looking all around the room instead of looking at the teacher and doing my work.
SP:	What else?
Kevin:	Sometimes I talk during reading time when I'm supposed to be quiet.
SP:	So you move around in your seat and talk and look

	around the room sometimes instead of looking at the teacher.
Kevin:	Yeah.
SP:	Tell me about a time when you were able to look at the teacher more or get more work done in class.

The use of videotalk shifted Kevin's attention from the vague labels of ADHD and "hyper" to the concrete behaviors of completing more class work and looking at the teacher more often. Diagnostic terms like ADHD and Oppositional Defiant Disorder (ODD) have become commonplace in schools and other agencies that serve children. Although diagnosis is still necessary in many settings for students to receive the services they need, diagnostic labels become disempowering when they begin to define the students themselves. Labels cannot tell us what *this* particular student is doing or not doing that constitutes a problem.

The next illustration involves Kendra, a 14-year-old student referred for disruptive behavior in the classroom and hallways.

Kendra:	I'm always getting in trouble at school.
School Practitioner (SP):	Getting in trouble. What does that look like?
Kendra:	I don't know. It just seems like I'm in trouble all the time.
SP:	It must be tough to be in trouble all the time.
Kendra:	It's been that way for a long time. Maybe it'll never change, I don't know.
SP:	So, you've been in trouble a lot and you feel like it would be really hard to change.
Kendra:	I don't know if I can do it.
SP:	It sounds like it would definitely be hard work. I wonder if you could help me get a better idea of your situation. Can you tell me about a time when you got in trouble at school this week?
Kendra:	Well, this morning I kicked the garbage can when I was walking out of science class. The trash came out a little on the floor. I picked it up, but my teacher still wrote me up and sent me to the office. Now I have two days of detention.
SP:	Okay. What are some other things that get you in trouble at school?

With some gentle prompting, Kendra was able to translate "getting in trouble at school" into changeable behaviors. This conversation illustrates two other advantages of talking with students about problems. First, the discussion of Kendra's problem provided the opportunity to acknowledge and validate her discouragement ("It must be tough to be in trouble all the time"). Second, the practitioner was able to use the language of qualification to invite a more hopeful outlook ("So, you've been in trouble a lot and you feel like it would be really hard to change").

Exploring Environmental Factors

School behavior problems do not exist in a vacuum, but are part of a larger environment consisting of people, places, and actions. A change in any aspect of the environment can help resolve the problem. This may include changes in: (a) the student, peers, teachers, or parents; (b) the classroom setting in which the problem typically occurs; or (c) the events and actions that immediately precede and follow the problem.

Exploring the environmental features of a problem may provide valuable clues for changing it. Several features of school problems are described below along with questions that we can ask ourselves, students, and others involved with the problem.

When?

Some school problems occur more regularly at specific times of the day, week, month, or year. The following questions are useful in clarifying any such patterns:

- Does this happen more in the morning or afternoon?
- Are there certain times of the day that are worse (or better) than others?
- Have things been better, worse, or about the same during the past week? … month? … year?

Where?

The following questions explore links between the problem and specific settings at school:

- Does the problem usually occur in a certain place (classroom, lunchroom, or hallway)?
- Are things better/worse in one class compared to others?
- Where is this problem most likely to happen?

With Whom?

Some problems vary in the presence of different people, which can be explored through the following questions:

- Who is usually around when the problem occurs?
- Does the problem occur most/least often with one particular teacher?
- Does the problem change depending on who you are around?

What Happens Right Before and After?

The questions below explore environmental antecedents and consequences of problem behavior:

- What is usually happening right before the problem?
- What are you usually doing right before the problem happens?

■ Is the problem more likely to occur during a certain type of activity (group discussion, individual seatwork)?
■ What usually happens right after the problem occurs?
■ How do your teachers respond? What do they say and do?
■ How do the other students respond?

Information from these questions can be used to build solutions by altering the school environment in some way. Let's look at two quick examples. If Lisa's problems typically involve a particular student who sits next to her in several classes, then changing the seating arrangement might help her behave better. If Miguel usually misbehaves shortly after arriving to school every morning, he could be encouraged to alter one small aspect of his morning routine—for example, he could walk directly to his desk and count silently to 20 upon entering the classroom, or his teacher might ask him to help with a chore when he walks into the classroom. Sometimes a small change in the environment is all that is required to pave the way for a solution.

Clarifying the Problem's Influence

Problems affect different students in different ways. After-school detention may be viewed by one student as a minor inconvenience and by another as a serious problem. The manner in which the problem impacts a particular student has major implications for how we approach the student.

One mistake that is often made in working with students is to assume that we know how the problem influences them. We are always better off to ask rather than assume. The following questions are useful in clarifying the influence of the problem on the student:

■ How does this problem affect your life at school and home?
■ How is it a problem for you?
■ How does it affect your relationship with your friends or teachers or parents?
■ What kind of hold does this problem have on you? How much power does it have over you?
■ How would your life be different without the problem?
■ If I asked your teachers or parents how this problem affects you, what would they say?

These questions serve at least two purposes. First, they prevent us from assuming anything or jumping to conclusions about the meaning and influence of the problem for the student. Second, they encourage the student to think about how the problem affects his or her life. I have found that students become more motivated to resolve a problem when they reflect on its power and influence in their lives. I recall an initial interview with a sensitive 13-year-old student named Isabella, who was genuinely moved and surprised by how strongly the problem affected her life after discussing a few of the questions listed above. She even took time to write this letter after our meeting:

Dear Dr. John: Thank you for talking to me last week. I'm going to try to be better at school because it's my life and nobody can do it for me. I have to do it for myself. If I don't do better, I won't have a chance to play basketball in middle school. My problems are hard on my mom, too. She has had a hard life but she is good to me. I don't want to make any more trouble for her. Thank you, Isabella

Our conversation prompted Isabella to consider the impact of the school problem in her life, which increased her commitment to take action.

Exploring Previous Solution Attempts

People typically struggle with a school problem for a long time before asking for help. In the course of the struggle, it is easy to become entranced by the problem and overlook potential solutions. Exploring attempted solutions helps us to (a) discover and apply what has already worked in addressing the problem or similar problems (successful attempts) and (b) discover and avoid what has not worked (unsuccessful attempts). This section provides a rationale for exploring previous solution attempts along with questions for doing so.

Have you ever struggled with a problem for a long time before recalling a strategy that helped you in a similar situation? When this happens to me, I am always surprised—and a little irritated—that I did not remember the strategy earlier. In addition to reminding students of previously successful strategies, exploring solution attempts helps to identify ineffective actions that might be contributing to the very problem they are intended to resolve. The following questions are useful in exploring previous solution attempts:

- What types of things have you already tried? How did they work?
- Of all the things that have been tried, what has worked the best?
- How have you handled similar challenges, and how could that help you with the problem you're having now?
- What have you thought about doing but haven't yet tried?
- What have other people done to help you? How did it work?

For students who have received prior counseling or intervention services, we can ask what was most and least helpful:

- What did the counselor do that worked well (or not so well) for you?
- Of all your experiences in counseling, what has helped you the most? How did you turn that into something that was helpful to you?
- What was most helpful/least helpful in your previous counseling experiences?
- What advice do you have for professionals who work with young people?

The following conversation illustrates the usefulness of exploring students' previous experiences in counseling and other services. This excerpt is taken from the first meeting with April, a 16-year-old referred by her mother and teachers due to oppositional behavior and declining grades.

School Practitioner (SP):	Your mother said that you met with a counselor last year.
April:	(Rolls her eyes.) Oh, yeah.
SP:	How did that go?
April:	Not real good. I hated going, especially at first, but my mom made me.
SP:	You said you hated it especially at first. Did it get any better after that?
April:	A little.
SP:	How often did you meet?
April:	We met once a week on Friday afternoon for a couple months. Friday afternoon! All my friends are getting ready for the weekend, and I had to go to see a shrink.
SP:	So the Friday afternoon thing was part of the problem.
April:	Yeah. I mean, why couldn't they pick another time? It was like they were punishing me.
SP:	Well, I can tell you we will not meet on Friday afternoon.
April:	Good.
SP:	Yeah, for me too. I want to be useful to you, and in order to do that, I need to know what was most helpful about the counseling or counselor, and what was not helpful. Can you help me with that?
April:	I can tell you what didn't help.
SP:	Okay. Thanks. What didn't help?
April:	Well, first of all, he would ask how things were going, and I would tell him. Then he would go on and on about something. You know, like things I should be doing and all. He would talk and talk and I'd just be sitting there. He was a nice guy and all, but …
SP:	So you wanted a chance to talk more?
April:	Yeah. I mean, not the whole time or anything, but how is it going to help me if I don't have a chance to talk?
SP:	Good point.
April:	He was a smart man. I know he cared and he was trying to help me.
SP:	How did you know he cared about you?
April:	I don't know. He would call sometimes during the week to check up on me and ask how things were going. It was cool that he did that.

SP: What else did he do that helped you or showed you that he cared?

As illustrated with April, students' feedback about what worked and did not work in previous counseling experiences provides useful tips about how to be most effective with them.

Exploring solution attempts invites students to stop and think about what they have already done, or might do differently, to address the problem. In addition to encouraging new ideas and actions, conversations about attempted solutions provide the opportunity to validate students' struggles and perceptions.

Exploring Students' Perceptions and Preferences

Action is always specific, concrete, individualized, and unique.

—John Dewey

One of the most practical features of the MRI brief strategic therapy approach (Fisch & Schlanger, 1999) is the emphasis on accommodating the client's "position." Position consists of a person's (a) perceptions of the problem and solution and (b) personal investment in resolving the problem.

The MRI group described three common positions in helping relationships: visitor, complainant, and customer. In the visitor-type relationship, clients are minimally invested in resolving the problem and may even see it as someone else's problem—students who may not even acknowledge that there is a problem in the first place, or may view it as their parent's or teacher's problem. In the complainant-type relationship, clients acknowledge that there is a problem but are unwilling to take any major actions to resolve it—students who admit that they need to improve school performance but are presently unable or unwilling to implement an improvement plan. The customer-type relationship is characterized by clients who acknowledge the problem and are willing to do something about it—students who are open to receiving advice and putting it into action at school.

I want to caution you against viewing one type of relationship or client as better than others. These categories can change quickly over the course of services and they are general guidelines to help practitioners work effectively with a wide range of students. Not surprisingly, the MRI group found that therapy was most successful when the practitioner cooperated with the client's position instead of trying to change it.

This section expands on the MRI notion of position and provides a host of strategies for clarifying students' perceptions regarding the problem, solution, and helping relationship. Most students who experience school problems have theories about their causes and solutions. They also have ideas and preferences about what is helpful to them and what they want from our services.

The following questions are useful in exploring students' perceptions related to the problem and solution:

- What do you think is causing this problem?
- If your teachers/parents/friends were here, what would they say causes the problem?
- What would they say would help to turn things around?
- What needs to happen for things to get better?
- What do you think would help improve things?
- Everyone has changed something. How does change usually happen in your life?

We can also learn about students' perceptions by paying careful attention to their language. One of the reasons I take notes is to record key words and phrases that reveal important aspects of a student's perspective. These words are useful in presenting interventions to students in ways that acknowledge their perceptions and engage their cooperation. In working with a student who complains about being "hassled" or "picked on" by the teacher, we could present an intervention strategy as a way to "get the teacher to stop hassling you."

The following conversation took place during the first meeting with Kasey, a 15-year-old student referred by her math teacher (Mr. Carter) because of disruptive classroom behavior. Kasey had already described several specific behaviors that comprised the problem. The following dialogue picks up with a question that explores Kasey's view of the situation.

School Practitioner (SP):	You know the situation better than anyone. How would you explain the problem in math class?
Kasey:	I can't stand Mr. Carter. He's always picking on me and I'm tired of it. I'm not putting up with it anymore. I don't care what he thinks of me.
SP:	You don't care what he says or thinks about you.
Kasey:	(Shakes head "no.") He doesn't like me, and I don't care what he thinks.
SP:	What else can you tell me to help me understand?
Kasey:	He has a big problem getting along with students. I'm not the only one. He's always saying we're lazy and we don't care about school.
SP:	So the main cause of the problem is that Mr. Carter picks on you. Is that it?
Kasey:	Yes. I'm not saying I'm an angel or anything like that, but I hate being picked on and he just keeps doing it.
SP:	No wonder you're having problems in there. He's picking on you, and you hate being picked on. That's a bad combination.
Kasey:	(Laughs.) It is.
SP:	Sounds like you're in a tough spot, Kasey. You need to pass the class, but that may not happen if things don't change soon. What needs to happen for things to get better?

Kasey:	He needs to stop picking on me.
SP:	Okay. What have you found helpful in getting him to pick on you less?
Kasey:	Nothing, really.
SP:	Nothing.
Kasey:	Well, when I just sit there and don't say anything, it helps a little.
SP:	You mean he picks on you less when you sit there and stay quiet?
Kasey:	Yes. But sometimes he does it anyway.
SP:	Okay. I think we're getting somewhere here. Sitting there and being quiet makes him pick on you less, which is what you want.
Kasey:	Right.
SP:	How would sitting there and being quiet affect your chances of passing the class?
Kasey:	What do you mean?
SP:	If you were quieter in class for the next week or two, would your chances of passing be better, worse, or about the same as they are right now.
Kasey:	Probably better. But why should I be good for him?
SP:	I wasn't thinking of him. I was thinking of you and your goal of passing, because you told me that you don't want to take the class all over again.
Kasey:	No way. With my luck I'd probably get him again. (Laughs.)

This discussion conveys respect for Kasey's perceptions through comments and questions such as, "You know the situation better than anyone" and "What else can you tell me to help me understand?" The practitioner not only explored Kasey's perspective, but invited her to examine the relationship between her actions and her goal of passing Mr. Carter's class. Kasey left the interview with her dignity intact and with a commitment to pass the class "no matter what he does or thinks of me."

Another aspect of exploring students' perspectives involves determining what they expect from practitioners and the helping relationship. Research supports the cooperative practice of matching our services to the preferences and expectations of those being served (Norcross, 2010). Students are more likely to participate with someone who is genuinely interested in their perceptions and preferences. Some students want a sounding board and listener, others want expert advice, and some want to brainstorm and problem solve. Some are willing to try anything to resolve the problem, while others see it as someone else's problem. Each student requires a customized approach that accommodates their perceptions and preferences. Adapting our approach and methods to the students we serve is also consistent with the American Psychological Association's (2006, p. 273) most recent definition of evidence-based practice as "the integration of the best available research with clinical expertise in the context of patient characteristics, culture, and preferences."

The following questions can be used in conjunction with the Session Rating Scale (discussed in Chapter 4) to determine what students want from our services:

- How can I help you with your goal of [student's stated goal]?
- What can we do in these meetings to make things better at school?
- Who has helped you the most with other concerns or problems in your life? What do they do that is most helpful?
- Since you were forced to come here and meet with me, would you be interested in working on ways to get out of having to come here?
- How can I help get your parents and teachers off your case about school?

Given the powerful influence of the client-practitioner alliance on outcomes (Norcross, 2010), accommodating what students want from us is one of the most important tasks of student-driven interviewing. Even though students are considered the primary clients of school services, their views are often overlooked when it comes to developing goals and interventions. This may occur because they are usually referred for services by teachers or parents. There is nothing more futile than trying to convince students to implement goals or strategies that are unimportant to them, regardless of how important they are to others. As illustrated in this chapter, cooperating with students' perceptions and preferences strengthens the therapeutic alliance and enhances outcomes. Table 7.1 summarizes and illustrates the strategies for discussing problems in solution-focused ways.

Summary and Conclusions

This chapter offers strategies for exploring students' perspectives on problems in ways that promote solutions—that is, talking about problems in solution-focused ways. There is a big difference between talking about a problem and becoming bogged down by it. Inviting students to describe problems in clear, observable terms (videotalk) results in changeable problems that are more amenable to intervention than vaguely stated problems or diagnoses such as immaturity or ADHD. Determining when and where problems typically occur helps to identify environmental elements that might be altered to promote solutions. Information about previous solution attempts provides important clues about what to do and not do in our work with students. Most students who experience behavior problems have theories about their causes and potential solutions, and these theories provide direction in selecting and presenting interventions that are acceptable to students. Students also have expectations and ideas about what is helpful to them and what they want from our services. Acknowledging students' perceptions and preferences lays the groundwork for helping them to develop useful goals, which is the topic of Chapter 8.

TABLE 7.1 Strategies for Discussing Problems in Solution-Focused Ways

Strategy	Description	Example
Acknowledging and prioritizing students' concerns	Accepting students' concerns and perceptions at face value; prioritizing students' concerns from their perspective	"Of all the concerns, which one is most important to you?"; "What do you want to work on first?"; [Pointing to the student's completed Outcome Rating Scale] "Which of these areas is most important to you right now?"
Describing changeable problems	Obtaining concrete descriptions of the problem ("videotalk")	Student: "I'm too hyper and disorganized". Practitioner: "What would I see if I videotaped you being hyper and disorganized in class?"
Exploring environmental factors	Identifying environmental events and conditions associated with the problem and potential solutions	"When, where, and with whom does the problem typically occur?"; "What happens right before and after the problem occurs?"
Clarifying the problem's influence	Determining how the problem impacts students' lives	"How has this affected your life at home or school?"; "What would your life be like without this problem?"; "How much power does this problem have in your life?"
Exploring previous solution attempts	Exploring attempted solutions and their relative success	"What types of things have you already tried? How did they work?"; "Of all the things that have been tried, what has worked the best/least?"
Exploring students' perceptions and preferences	Exploring students' theories and position on the problem and potential solutions; Clarifying what students expect from you and your services	"What do you think is causing this problem?"; "What will help you turn it around and make things better at school?"; "What can I do, and we do, in these meetings to make this time as useful as possible for you?"

Reflection and Application

1. Think of a concern or problem in your life, and practice the following tasks: (a) Define the concern in concrete terms using videotalk; (b) describe environmental factors related to the problem (when, where, with whom); (c) list previous solution attempts and their effectiveness; and (d) describe your theory of the problem and solution. Using information from the above items, list one or two actions that you are willing to take next week to change the problem.

2. This exercise provides practice in helping people describe their concerns using videotalk. Pair up with a partner and assume the roles of student and practitioner. Carry out the following tasks in about ten minutes: (a) The student describes a school problem in vague and global terms; and (b) the practitioner asks questions aimed at eliciting a more concrete, specific description of the problem. When you finish one round, switch roles and repeat the exercise.

3. Clarifying the influence of school problems upon the lives of students helps us to better understand their perspectives. To gain first-hand experience with this strategy, select a current concern in your life and ask yourself the following questions aimed at clarifying the impact of the problem on you and your life: (a) How is it a problem for you?; (b) in what specific way(s) does it affect your contentment or quality of life?; (c) how does it block you from being more like the person you want to be?; and (d) how would your life be different without the problem? After answering these questions, take a moment to consider how your responses affect your commitment and motivation to resolve the problem.

4. Exploring solution attempts helps students to remember and use what has worked, to avoid what has not worked, and to consider what else they could do to address a problem. To obtain a more personalized experience in exploring solution attempts, think of a problem that you have struggled with and ask yourself the following questions: (a) Of all the things you have done to address the problem, what has been most effective?; (b) what has been least effective?; and (c) what have you thought about doing but haven't yet done? Use your responses to list one specific action that you can take next week to improve the situation.

5. Pair up with a partner to practice the strategy of exploring people's perceptions and preferences by assuming the roles of client and practitioner as you carry out the following steps: (a) client briefly describes a concern; (b) practitioner acknowledges the client's struggle and explores his or her perceptions of the problem and solution; and (c) practitioner explores the client's preferences about the helping relationship. Switch roles and repeat the exercise.

6. Describe one small step that you are willing to take in your work with students as a result of the information in this chapter.

eight
Creating Goals That Matter

Chapter Objectives

- To highlight the prominent role of goals in building solutions;
- To emphasize the importance of involving students in creating goals that matter;
- To describe five features of effective goals;
- To illustrate practical strategies for developing goals with a variety of students.

We may need to solve problems not by removing the cause, but by designing the way forward.

— Edward de Bono

Goals are the driving force of effective action. They provide the purpose and hope that helps students persevere and stay on track in the face of obstacles and setbacks. This chapter describes practical strategies for collaborating with students to develop goals that matter and motivate.

Goals as Maps, Practitioners as Travel Agents

If you don't know where you're going, you might wind up someplace else.

— Yogi Berra

A clear goal is to solution building what a clear map is to navigation. A good map does not guarantee success, but a vague map or no map at all almost always guarantees failure. Like a good map, a clear goal helps students and practitioners stay on track and move in a purposeful direction.

The extent to which students and practitioners agree on goals strongly influences outcomes—the better the agreement, the better the outcome (Tryon & Winograd, 2011). One way to ensure close agreement on goals is to view ourselves as travel agents (Murphy, 2010). Effective travel agents find out exactly where their clients want to go before offering any suggestions or travel plans. The only way to know where students want to go—and how they prefer to get there—is to involve them in every aspect of goal development.

The Importance of Student Involvement

Tell me, I forget. Involve me, I understand.

—Chinese proverb

Involving clients in the development of therapeutic goals enhances their motivation to reach them (Rollnick, Miller, & Butler, 2008). Sadly, students are often excluded from the goal-building process. Adults may spend considerable time talking among themselves without ever consulting the student. Some students are viewed as incapable of contributing to goal development due to their age, developmental level, or other discounting assumptions. Adults may also make the mistake of assuming that students are motivated by the same goals that motivate them—or the same goals that motivated them when they were students.

Excluding or minimizing the student's input is like rowing a boat with one paddle instead of two. Like the boat with one paddle, our work with students will turn in circles unless they are actively involved in developing personally meaningful goals.

Features of Effective Goals: The 5-S Guideline

Effective goals share several common features. The 5-S guideline (Murphy, 2008) is a helpful way of remembering the five characteristics of useful goals: Significant, specific, small, start-based, and self-manageable. Each of these characteristics is discussed below.

Significant

Strong reasons make strong actions.

—William Shakespeare

Science can tell us what works, but it can't tell us what to work on. Choosing therapeutic goals—that is, *what* to work on—is a deeply personal issue for each student. The most important aspect of a school-related goal is its personal significance to the student. Unfortunately, this consideration often takes a back seat to the preferences of helping professionals, teachers, parents, administrators—everyone except the student. Regardless of what others think, a school goal must mean something to students in order to engage their investment and motivation. Box 8.1 invites you to explore this issue in your own life.

Box 8.1 How Important Is it to You?

1. Think of a significant goal or project in your personal or work life.
2. Now think of a less important goal or project that you are involved in.
3. How does your motivation and commitment differ for these two goals/projects? What are some other key differences in your approach to these two goals/projects?

Student-driven interviewing enhances students' motivation by helping them develop personally significant and meaningful goals or "goals that matter."

Developing goals that matter requires us to determine what matters most to students—key values in their lives—and how school fits into their values. Students do not automatically connect their school performance to larger values and visions, and helping them make these connections can enhance their school-related motivation and involvement. Specific methods for doing so are addressed later in the chapter.

Specific

Students sometimes describe their goals in abstract terms such as being less depressed, doing better at school, or improving their attitude. These goals are much more difficult to envision, measure, and reach than concrete goals such as arriving to school on time or improving grades. It is not surprising that specific goals lead to higher energy and performance levels than vague goals (Halvorson, 2010). After all, it is much easier to measure and know exactly how many days you arrived to work or school on time for one week than it is to know exactly how depressed or mature or responsible you've been during the week.

When students use vague language, we can invite them to describe the same goals using videotalk. Students who want to "improve their attitude" can be asked, "What would I see if I watched a videotape of you with a better attitude at school?" In the brief dialogue that follows, the practitioner requests a videotalk description of "doing better in school" to assist Hector, age 10, in developing a more specific goal.

School Practitioner (SP): How will you know when you start doing a little better in school, Hector?

Hector: What do you mean?

SP:	Let's pretend we tape record you doing better in school (practitioner mimics holding a small recording device), okay?
Hector:	Okay.
SP:	Now we push the play button and we see you doing better at school. Tell me what we will see you doing when we watch this.
Hector:	I'm sitting down and answering questions in class like everyone else. And I'm smiling because I got all the words right on my spelling test.
SP:	Okay. What else would we see?
Hector:	I'm handing my homework in and my teacher tells me I got them all right.

As illustrated with Hector, helping students translate vague goals ("being good" or "doing better" at school) into specific, observable descriptions makes it easier for practitioners and students to monitor progress and notice small improvements. Research also suggests that concrete goals can increase people's sense of energy and optimism in pursuit of such goals (Snyder, Lopez, Shorey, Rand, & Feldman, 2003).

Small

If you want to move a mountain, start with the first pebble.
—Chinese Proverb

As runners and mountain climbers will tell you, success results from breaking large goals such as mountain summits and finish lines into a series of smaller goals, which might be the first few steps up a mountain or the next mile of a marathon. Just as mountain climbers may be overwhelmed by the thought of scaling a steep and rough cliff, the thought of changing a large school problem can be overwhelming to students. For this reason, it is helpful to focus on small changes instead of trying to tackle too much right away. The following questions encourage students to focus on small, manageable changes:

- What will be the first small sign that things are getting better?
- What are one or two tiny steps that you're willing to take next week to move a little closer to your goal of passing science class?
- If a score of 100 was "where you want things to be" and 10 was "where things are right now," what would a 12 or 15 look like?
- (Responding to the student's ratings on the Child Outcome Rating Scale) Your score on the school scale is 5.4. What will a 5.5 look like?

Some students express extremely high expectations when asked about their goals. For example, a student who is failing most classes may want to become an honor roll student by the end of the semester. I would never rule out the possibility, but I would encourage the student to concentrate on the first couple of steps toward becoming an honor roll student. In the following conversation with a 14-year-old student named Cheryl, the school practitioner acknowledges Cheryl's hope of raising her science grade from a D to an A while encouraging her to focus on one small step at a time.

School Practitioner (SP):   So you want to raise your grade from a D to an A by the end of the semester, which is two months from now. That sounds like it's going to take some hard work. What do you need to do to make it happen?

Cheryl: I have to do a lot better.

SP: Tell me one small thing you could do tomorrow to move a little closer to a better grade.

Cheryl: I guess I could work on my semester project because that's a big part of our grade.

SP: When is the last time you worked on this project?

Cheryl: (Laughs.) It was a long time ago.

SP: Okay, so it's been a while. Are you willing to set aside five minutes tomorrow during study hall to work on the project?

Cheryl: I can do more than five minutes.

SP: That's fine, but five minutes would be an important step because it's been so long since you've worked on it. Are you willing to do that tomorrow?

After acknowledging Cheryl's ambitious goal of earning an A, the practitioner invited her to focus on one small step toward her goal. I think it is important for young people to think big when it comes to their hopes and aspirations. Most people—whether they are runners, mountain climbers, or students—have the best chance of reaching their final goal when they focus on the next few steps of the journey.

Start-Based

When asked what they want from services, students often tell us what they don't want: "I want to be less depressed" or "I want to stop getting in trouble." These statements describe the absence or reduction of a problem with no indication of what students want instead. Goals that are worded in positive, start-based language ("arriving to school on time" or "taking more notes during class") are more measurable and motivating than negatively worded goals. Consider how difficult it is to observe the absence of depression or anxiety. What does "non-depression" look like and how will you know when it happens? From a functional standpoint, the most effective way to change a problem behavior is to replace it with a productive behavior (Watson & Steege, 2009). So, rather than simply reducing the number of times Michael leaves his seat in class, we can teach him what to do instead of leaving his seat—working on class assignments, listening to the teacher, and so forth. Start-based goals are based on the same idea.

In addition to being more measurable, start-based goals focus students' attention toward future solutions rather than past problems. Diagnostic language can hamper the development of start-based goals. When students describe themselves or their problems in diagnostic terms, such as saying "I was just being ADHD," we can ask, "What would you be doing differently at school if you weren't being ADHD?" This question encourages start-based goals by inviting students to focus on the presence or increase of desired behavior.

Self-Manageable

I'm the boss of me, right?

—Adam, 12-year-old student

The following statements are familiar to many school practitioners:

- Things would be fine if my teachers would just back off.
- I wouldn't have any problems if other kids would leave me alone.
- My teachers don't like me, so why should I even try?
- The teacher is a control freak, and she is always looking to get me in trouble.

The way that we talk about a problem or solution strongly influences our thoughts, hopes, and actions. Statements that focus on the attitudes or behavior of other people—such as those listed above—draw attention away from the student's role in school solutions by focusing on people and circumstances over which the student has little control. As illustrated in the following dialogue with a 15–year-old named Ron, we can respect students' perceptions while inviting them to consider what they can do to improve the situation.

Ron:	Most of the teachers here pick on me all the time in class.
School Practitioner (SP):	That must be tough for you. What do you usually say or do when they pick on you? [shifting the focus from teachers to Ron.]
Ron:	I try to shut it out.
SP:	How do you do that?
Ron:	I just do it.
SP:	If I was in class watching you shut it out, what would I see? [requesting videotalk.]
Ron:	I just look the other way and pretend they're not talking to me.
SP:	What do they do then?
Ron:	Nothing, sometimes. Most of the time they get mad and they say I don't care about school.
SP:	Is that true? [shifting attention back to Ron.]
Ron:	No. I know I'm not the smartest student and I can get pretty worked up, but they don't know anything about

	me and they go off saying all this stuff and it makes me mad. How do they know whether or not I care about school?
SP:	Good point.
Ron:	They've never even talked to me, so how do they know what I think about school? It's not that I don't care about school. I want to get my credits and get out of here.
SP:	So it's important that you not fail and lose any credits this year?
Ron:	Yes. I don't want to be here any longer than I have to. (Laughs.)
SP:	That makes sense. How willing are you to put your goal of passing your classes to the test by trying an experiment? [staying focused on Ron and his goal.]
Ron:	Like what?
SP:	I don't know. But I wonder what would happen if you did something very different the next time one of your teachers picks on you. Maybe we can come up with something in the next few minutes. It would be like doing an experiment in one or two of your classes to see what would happen when you do something different. [inviting Ron to embrace the self-manageable goal of responding differently in class.]
Ron:	I'm not sure about that. What if they get madder?
SP:	That's a good point. I guess you'll never know unless you try it. It's up to you, but it might be interesting to see what happens.

The 5-S guideline is a helpful way to remember the five key features of effective goals—significant, specific, small, start-based, and self-manageable. These features are summarized and illustrated in Table 8.1.

Strategies for Developing Useful Goals

This section outlines specific techniques for helping students develop clear and meaningful goals.

Linking School Performance to Students' "Big Values"

> Why should I change just because THEY think I should?
>
> —Cara, 15-year-old student

The term "values" is used here to refer to the purpose, meaning, and vision that students hold for their lives. I believe that the role of values in school-based intervention has been largely untapped, and that the failure to consider students'

TABLE 8.1   Features of Effective Goals: The 5-S Guideline

Feature	Description	Sample Questions
Significant	Personally relevant and meaningful; compatible with students' "big values"	"What do you want your life to stand for, and how does school figure into that?"; "What is most important to you?"
Specific	Clear, observable "action descriptions" and "videotalk"	"If I videotaped you being better at school, what would I see?"; "What will you do differently when you 'change your attitude' at school?"
Small	Attainable "first steps" in the right direction	"What will be the first small sign that things are getting a little better at school?"; "What will it take to move your rating from a 2 to a 2.1 or 2.2?"
Start-based	The "start of" or presence of desirable actions	"What will you be doing instead of acting up in class?"; "How would you act if you weren't ADHD?"
Self-manageable	Within the student's control	"How willing are you to try something different?"; "What can you do to improve your grades?"

values jeopardizes the relevance and effectiveness of our services. For some students, school performance holds little intrinsic value or interest. Lacking a personal reason to do well in school, students may understandably adopt a "what's the use?" or "why should I even try?" position.

One way to link students' values to their school performance is to enlarge the conversation beyond the scope of school. Inviting students to reflect on their deepest values creates a meaningful and personally relevant context for discussing school goals. Goals that lack personal relevance for students are doomed to fail for the same reason that I don't put much effort into goals that are not sufficiently meaningful or motivating for me. Box 8.2 provides an opportunity to reflect on the impact of values in your life.

Values provide a meaning-rich context for developing goals that matter to students. The following questions invite students to reflect on their deepest values and visions:

■ Let's forget about school for a few minutes. If you could be just the kind of person you most want to be, what kind of person is that?

■ What do you want your life to stand for?

■ Pretend that you are 50 years old and that your life has turned out just the way you wanted it to be. Now imagine picking up a book called "Michelle's Life," and reading your life story at age 50. What are the most important parts of the story?

Box 8.2 Aligning Actions with Values

Take a few minutes to answer the following questions.

■ If you could choose to have your life be about something, what would it be?
■ What are the most important values in your life?
■ What are you already doing to support your strongest values and what would it take to do more of it?
■ What is currently blocking you from living in ways that are more compatible with your values?
■ On a scale of 1 (not very willing) to 10 (very willing), how willing are you to take action toward bringing your life in closer alignment with your values?
■ What small step are you willing to take tomorrow to live out your values more fully?

We can ask students similar questions to help them align their school behavior with their biggest hopes and values.

Once values are identified, we can encourage students to (a) reflect on the relationship between their values and school-related actions, and (b) make behavioral commitments and changes that support their values. It is helpful to use students' actual words whenever. The following questions invite students to act on their deepest values at school and elsewhere:

■ What are you already doing at school to help yourself become the *decent person* you want to be? What will it take to do more of that?
■ If you were doing what you needed to do in school to become a more *decent person*, what would it be?
■ What do you need to do differently at school to prepare you for being *a good husband and father* when you get older?
■ If it were possible for you to have *a better life*, would you be willing to change some things at school to make it happen?

Values must be translated into specific actions to be of any use in helping students resolve problems. Aligning school-related goals with students' values increases their motivation, accountability, and investment in the change process. The more invested students are in building solutions, the more likely they will be to maintain positive behaviors after formal intervention has ended and to generalize these behaviors to other settings (Goldstein & Martens, 2000).

Asking Future-Focused Miracle Questions

You can never plan the future by the past.

—Edmund Burke

The miracle question helps students develop goals by having them envision and describe a problem-free future. de Shazer (1988) first formulated the question in this way: "Suppose that one night, while you were asleep, there was a miracle and this problem was solved. How would you know? What would be different?" (p. 5). Variations of the question include the following:

- Let's say a miracle happens while you are sleeping tonight and this problem is completely solved. What would be different at school tomorrow? What would your teacher notice?
- If the problem suddenly vanished, what would be the first small sign that things were different at school tomorrow?
- Let's pretend that you had a dream last night and the problem was solved during the dream. How was it solved? What did you do to help solve it?

Visual images and metaphors can be incorporated into miracle-type questions to engage students' attention and help them to picture and describe life without the problem:

- If someone waved a magic wand and made this problem disappear, how would you be able to tell things were different at school?
- Imagine that we are looking into a crystal ball at a time in the future when this problem no longer occurs at school. What do you see?
- Pretend that you are at school after the miracle and show me what you will be doing differently in math class. I can be the teacher and you can tell me what I should be doing.
- Imagine that there are two movies about your life. Movie #1 is about your life with the problem, and Movie #2 is about your life without the problem. I already know a lot about Movie #1. Tell me what Movie #2 would look like. Who would be in it? What would they be doing?
- Pretend that you are the captain of a space ship flying to a planet called Future Land where school is just the way you want it to be and there are never any problems. Tell me how your school life would be different in Future Land.

Props and imaginary characters can be used with young children. For example, children can describe what school is like after a genie emerges from a magic lamp and frees them from the problem. A magic wand (pencil), crystal ball (anything round), problem-vanishing dust (from a bookshelf), and other simple devices can be incorporated into the miracle question to engage children's interest and involvement. As illustrated next with David—a 12-year-old student referred for classroom behavior problems—it is helpful to obtain as much detail as possible about students' vision of a better future.

School Practitioner (SP):	Suppose a miracle occurred one night while you were sleeping and this problem vanished. What would be different at school?
David:	I wouldn't have detention.
SP:	What else?

David:	My grades would be better.
SP:	What else would be different at school or home?
David:	My parents wouldn't be talking about school all the time. That would be a big miracle.

Instead of stopping after David's first response, the practitioner obtained a more complete description by asking what else would be different after the miracle. The following excerpts illustrate how practitioners can follow up the miracle question to create effective goals based on the 5-S guideline.

School Practitioner (SP):	David, when I asked you the miracle question, you said that you wouldn't have detention and your grades would improve. That sounds like someone who cares and wants school to be better. Why is school important to you?
David:	You have to do good enough in school to get a job after high school.
SP:	That makes sense. Why is it important for you to get a decent job? [This question invites David to consider the personal significance of getting a job, which lays the groundwork for developing school-related goals that link his current school performance to future job prospects. The dialogue picks up a few minutes later as David and the practitioner flesh out his goals by addressing other features of the 5-S guideline.]
SP:	You mentioned that you wouldn't get in trouble or have detention after the miracle. What could you do differently to stay out of trouble and detention? [This question promotes start-based goals by encouraging David to think about the start of desirable actions rather than the absence of undesirable ones.]
David:	Pay attention to my teachers and do my work. And get better grades.
SP:	What would I see if I videotaped you paying attention to your teacher? [Requesting a videotalk description promotes a specific, observable goal.]
David:	I'd be looking at the teacher and taking some notes instead of looking at my friends or out the window.
SP:	Which one of these things would you be willing to work on first, even just a little, during the next couple days at school? [This question keeps David in the driver's seat by asking for his opinion on what to work on first. The phrase "even just a little" invites him to focus on small changes instead of the more overwhelming task of changing everything all at once.]

David:	I guess taking notes because it would help my grades.
SP:	That makes sense. What is one small thing you could do next week to get closer to where you want to be on taking notes? [This question encourages David to commit to a small, specific goal.]
	[Later in the conversation ...]
SP:	You said that you want your parents to stop asking so many questions about school. I wonder what you could do to get them to ask fewer questions about school. [This statement paves the way for self-manageable goals by inviting David to consider what he could do to reduce his parents' questions about school.]

As seen with David, the miracle question helps create a student-driven context for developing practical goals based on the 5-S guideline. The opportunity to focus on a better future can be a breath of fresh air for students who are burdened by ongoing problems at school. Inviting students to imagine and describe a better future lays the groundwork for developing meaningful goals and action plans. Most young people enjoy the playful nature of the miracle question, but no single technique works with every student. Some may view the miracle question as impractical or irrelevant. When this happens, we can simply accept their response and move on to other goal development strategies.

Asking Scaling Questions

> Numbers constitute the only universal language.
>
> —Nathanael West

Scaling strategies serve many purposes in student-driven interviews, one of which is to help students develop goals as illustrated by the following questions:

- On a scale from 0 to 10, with 10 being the best that things could be and 0 being the worst, where would you rate things in your science class right now? What would the next highest number look like?
- What will you do differently when you move from a 3 to a 3.5 or 4? How will your teachers/parents be able to tell you moved up a little?
- If I videotaped you after you have moved up one point, what would I see?
- [Responding to the student's ratings on the Child Outcome Rating Scale] Your mark on the family scale was 5.8. What will a 6 look like?

Scaling questions can be presented in different formats depending on the student's age and abilities. In working with younger students, you can use a row of blocks, a series of faces, or a line on a piece of paper. Here are a few examples:

- Show the child five blocks and say, "I want to know how things are going in school right now." Arrange the blocks in a row or tower and say, "This (pointing to the entire row or stack of blocks) means things are really great and just the way you want them to be at school, and this (pointing to only one block) means things are really bad. Use the blocks to show me how things are going for you at school right now." Pencils, paper clips, or other available objects can also be used for this purpose.

■ Draw a vertical line on a piece of paper and say, "If this bottom part shows where you would be if you got into trouble all the time at school, and this top part shows where you would be if things were perfect at school and you never got in trouble, show me where you are right now." After the student marks a spot on the line, we can help them construct a small goal by pointing to a spot slightly above the student's mark and asking what will be different at school when the mark moves a little higher.

■ Tailoring the scale to students' unique interests is another way to enhance their comprehension of scaling questions. In working with a student who loves football, for example, the scale can be presented as a football field broken into ten equal segments ranging from farthest away to nearest to the student's goal.

The Outcome Rating Scale (ORS; Miller & Duncan, 2000) is another scaling strategy that can be used to develop goals. As discussed in Chapter 4, the ORS requires students to rate how they are doing in different areas by marking a 10-centimeter line. When students mark the lines and identify key concerns, we can inquire about small steps toward their goals:

■ I can see that you're pretty concerned about school (pointing to the student's mark on the school scale). Tell me what needs to happen for this mark to go up to about here (pointing to a spot slightly above the student's mark).

■ Your score on the social scale is 4.6. What will a 4.8 or 5 look like?

■ You rated the family scale at a 6.8. What could you do to bring that up to a 6.9 or 7?

The form of the scale is less important than its function—to engage students in developing clear and reasonable goals. The following conversations show how scaling can be incorporated into goal-related conversations with students of all ages. The first example involves a 13-year-old student named Mysha, who was referred for talking back to teachers.

School Practitioner (SP):   On a scale of 0 to 100, where 100 is the very best that things can be at school and 0 is the very worst, where are things in school now?

Mysha: I'd say about 20.

SP: How will things be different at school when it moves to a 25?

Mysha: My social studies teacher and I won't be getting into it all the time.

SP:	Okay. What else?
Mysha:	My attitude will be a little better.
SP:	If I videotaped you with a better attitude, what would I see you doing differently at school?

In the example that follows, the practitioner uses hands-on materials and strategies with a 5-year-old student named Jake.

School Practitioner (SP):	(Lays out eight small buttons in a row on the table.) I want to know how things are going in school right now and we can use these buttons to help us talk about it. This (pointing to the eighth button) means things are really great at school and this (pointing to the first button) means things are really bad. Point to a button to show me how school is going for you.
Jake:	(Points to the second button in the row.)
SP:	So things are not too good at school for you?
Jake:	No, they aren't.
SP:	Okay. I wonder what school will look like when things are about here (pointing to third button). What's going to be different at school?
Jake:	I won't be so bad and I'll get to play with other kids more.
SP:	Do you want that to happen?
Jake:	(Nods "yes.")
SP:	Why is it important for you to get to play with other kids more?
Jake:	I like to play kickball and other stuff but I have to sit by the teacher and I don't get to play.
SP:	Okay. I'm sorry to hear that, Jake. How will your teacher know that you went from here (pointing to the second button)—the way things are now—up to here when they get a little better (pointing to third button)?
Jake:	I'll be nicer to her and other students.
SP:	How would you do that?
Jake:	I'll do what she tells me instead of getting mad.
SP:	What else would you be doing when you're here (pointing to third button)?

For students who are more comfortable with numbers than words, scaling provides a respectful way to explore their goals. Scaling strategies also add a novel and playful element, which is always a welcome addition when working with young people. Whatever the reason, many students respond better to the miracle and scaling questions than they do to more direct, traditional questions about their goals.

Asking "How Can I Help You?"

In addition to exploring students' values and asking miracle and scaling questions, we can initiate goal-related discussions by asking "How can I help you?" The practical simplicity of this question captures the essence of student-driven interviewing—being useful to students and respecting their opinions. Variations of the question include the following:

- How can I help you make things better at school?
- What can I do to help you?
- How will you know I'm being helpful to you?
- What will be different at school if our meetings are successful?

The following exchange occurred early in the first meeting with Yvonne, a 13-year-old middle school student.

School Practitioner (SP):	How can I help you at school?
Yvonne:	I don't know.
SP:	Since these meetings are about you and what you want to happen at school, I'm wondering what I could do or what we could do in these meetings to help you.
Yvonne:	Well, I have trouble concentrating in class. My mom says I daydream a lot because I think about other things instead of paying attention to teachers of what's going on in class.
SP:	Do you want to learn to concentrate better in class?
Yvonne:	Yes.
SP:	Is that something you want to work on in our meetings?
Yvonne:	I guess so.

Yvonne and the practitioner went on to discuss specific signs of concentrating in class such as fewer discipline referrals and higher grades on tests. The entire conversation evolved from asking Yvonne the simple question, "How can I help you?"

Incorporating Students' Language and Perceptions into Goals

We rarely confide in those who are better than we are.
—Albert Camus

School-related goals should reflect key words, phrases, and perceptions of the student whenever possible. This point applies to every student and every circumstance, but the following discussion addresses situations that are particularly challenging for practitioners—when students do not want to participate in services and when they perceive that their goals and preferences take a back seat to the wishes of teachers, parents, or others.

The fact that most students are referred to us by others has major implications for how we approach them about goals. Students have a sixth sense when it comes to detecting adults who ignore their opinions or try to talk them into different ways of thinking. Instead of calling students resistant or otherwise discounting their perspectives, we can meet them where they are by integrating their language and perceptions into goal-related discussions. In working with a student who wants to "get out of" counseling, we can ask, "What needs to happen for you to get out of having to come here?" The following questions invite so-called "reluctant students" to develop goals that accommodate their language and perceptions:

- I know you would rather not be here, so maybe we could work on getting you out of having to do that. Are you interested?
- On a scale of 1 to 100, where 1 is "I won't do anything" and 100 is "I'll do anything to get out of coming here," how would you rate your willingness to take action that helps you get out of counseling as soon as possible?
- Would you be interested in finding ways to keep your parents or teachers off your case about school?
- What would convince your teachers/parents that you no longer need counseling?
- I already know what your teachers and parents want to change, but what do *you* want to change?

The words of parents and teachers may differ significantly from the words of students in describing what they want from our services. A teacher may want the student to be "more respectful and responsible" whereas the student simply "wants to be left alone and hassled less" at school. We can cooperate with everyone involved by asking follow-up questions about specific actions that are associated with each person's goal. For the teacher: "What will it look like when Tim becomes more responsible?" For the student: "What will it take for teachers to leave you alone and hassle you less at school?" Both questions may lead to similar goals despite differences in their wording—the behaviors required to satisfy the teacher's goal of "respect and responsibility" are likely to meet the student's goal of "being left alone and hassled less at school." Accommodating people's language and perceptions helps to create goals that are respectful and acceptable to everyone involved.

Asking Social Relationship Questions

As noted in Chapter 5, social relationship questions invite students to reflect on the views of key people and the social impact of solutions. This section describes how social relationship questions can be used to promote goals that matter to students—even in situations when students view the problem as trivial or as belonging to someone else. Here are a few examples:

- Who do you respect the most in your life? What would he or she advise you to do about this problem at school?
- Of everyone involved with this problem, who is most concerned about it?

What would he or she suggest as a way to make things better for you at school?
- What would your teacher say if I asked what you could do to improve things at school?
- What advice would your best friend give you?

These questions invite students to consider the problem and solution from the perspectives of teachers, parents, and others—with no pressure to agree with or adopt their views. This broadens the student's frame of reference and creates new avenues of goal development and solution building. For example, students who discuss how a friend or favorite aunt would handle the school problem may change their approach to the problem as a result of the discussion.

Social relationship questions also invite students to reflect on the social impact of solutions as illustrated below:

- How will your teacher treat you differently when things start improving?
- How will your relationship with your parents change when the school stops calling them about your behavior?
- Let's pretend that you are not having any more problems at school. How would that change your life at school and home?
- If things improve a little at school, who will be the first to notice? How will he or she react? How would that be for you?
- What would your teacher do if you started doing more work in class?

Asking social relationship questions is always better than telling students how their lives will be better when their school behavior improves.

The following dialogue took place during the first meeting with a 13-year-old named Roz, who was referred for behavioral intervention by her history teacher, Ms. Bell. The conversation illustrates how social relationship questions help students create meaningful goals.

School Practitioner (SP):	Ms. Bell seems really concerned about your behavior.
Roz:	I know. She's always telling me "do this" and "do that" and "be respectful" and things like that.
SP:	Who is more concerned about your behavior, you or Ms. Bell?
Roz:	She is. I know I could do better, but why should I? Everything would be fine if she would just leave me alone.
SP:	How big of a hassle is it for you when she gets on your case?
Roz:	I hate it. I told her to stop bothering me.
SP:	How did that work?
Roz:	(Laughs.) Not too good.
SP:	What else have you tried to get her to stop hassling you?
Roz:	(Shrugs shoulders.) Nothing.

SP:	Okay. You know Ms. Bell a lot better than I do, so I have a question for you. What would Ms. Bell say if I asked her what you could do to get her off your case?
Roz:	She'd probably say that I should do more work and talk nicer to her and stop messing around in class.
SP:	What would happen if you were to do a little more work or talk a little nicer in class? How would that change things between you and Ms. Bell?
Roz:	I don't know if it would change anything. I'm not saying it wouldn't change anything. But she has her way of doing things and I'm not sure how much she would change.
SP:	If she would by chance change just a little, how might she treat you differently in class?
Roz:	I don't know. She might let me do more things.
SP:	What kind of things?
Roz:	Like jobs in the classroom, taking notes to other teachers, stuff like that.
SP:	Would you like to do more of those things?
Roz:	Yes, because you get to leave class instead of sitting there the whole time. And you don't get in trouble for it.
SP:	That makes sense. So, if you did more work and said a few nice things in class, then maybe you would have more freedom and have a better chance to do more of those jobs and errands that other students get to do. What do you think?
Roz:	(Nods "yes.") But I don't know if that's going to happen.
SP:	I don't either. How willing are you to try to make it happen, even just a little?
Roz:	I guess I could try.
SP:	What else might change for you at school or home if things get a little better in history class?

As illustrated with Roz, students may not fully consider the social consequences of improving school behavior unless they are directly asked about them. Many students are quick to acknowledge other people's influence on them while underestimating their own influence on others. Roz was well aware of Ms. Bell's impact on her. She was less aware yet more intrigued by the possibility that she might influence Ms. Bell's behavior by changing her own behavior.

Summary and Conclusions

Goals are the driving force of action and solutions. Students are capable of amazing changes and accomplishments when they are working toward goals that matter to them. The extent to which students participate in the development of goals strongly influences the success of our services. This chapter outlines several strategies for collaborating with students of all ages to construct goals that meet the 5-S guideline by being significant, specific, small, start-based, and self-manageable. These strategies include the miracle question, scaling, incorporating students' language and perceptions into goals, and asking social relationship questions. Once goals are in place, we can help students discover exceptions and other resources that can be applied toward school solutions. These strategies are addressed in the next two chapters.

Reflection and Application

1. Select two current clients and examine the extent to which the stated goals of your services meet the 5-S guideline of being significant, specific, small, start-based, and self-manageable. How might these goals be modified to align them more closely with the 5-S guideline?

2. Choose a current problem in your life and describe what would be different if a miracle occurred and the problem suddenly vanished. How could you or others tell that the miracle had occurred? Be thorough and specific in your description of life after the miracle. Of all those things that would be different, which ones are already happening, if only just a little? What needs to happen in order to increase or sustain these desired actions or events? What are you willing to do to make this happen?

3. Think of a problem or concern in your life and rate it on a scale from 0 to 10, with 0 being "the worst it could be" and 10 being "the best it can be." What would a half step higher look like? Be specific. Describe what you or others will be doing when things get a little better. How will this be for you? Reflect on the following questions after you complete the exercise: (a) How did this exercise affect your approach to the problem and solution?; (b) How did it influence your thoughts and views of your goal?; and (c) How did it affect your hope about future improvements?

4. Select a current (or previous) client and consider the extent to which the stated goal reflects (or reflected) the client's language and perceptions. List a couple of ways that you can incorporate students' language and perceptions into the process of school-related goals.

5. Practice social relationship questions by pairing up with a partner and assuming the roles of client and helper. Have the client share a concern or problem, then ask a few social relationship questions aimed at helping the client formulate a clear goal (What would your best friend advise you to do about this?) and reflect on the social impact of reaching the goal (Who would be the first to notice the change, and how might they respond?).

6. Describe one small step that you are willing to take in your work with students as a result of the information in this chapter.

nine

Working with What Works

I: Non-Problems

Chapter Objectives

- To define exceptions to the problem (non-problems);
- To discuss the benefits of identifying and increasing exceptions;
- To describe practical strategies for identifying and increasing exceptions with a variety of students.

I didn't know I was doing anything right.

—Erika, 8-year-old student

It immediately caught my eye as I looked over the referral form from Ms. Kent, a fourth-grade teacher who requested assistance with one of her students. The first question asked for a problem description and reason for referral. Ms. Kent's response filled the space beneath the question and half of a second sheet of paper that was attached to the referral form. Her response to the next item, which inquired about the student's strengths, included two words—beautiful hair. This is a striking example of the difference between people's response to problem-based and strength-based questions. But Ms. Kent is not alone. Her responses illustrate a common tendency of people who are struggling with difficult problems—a tendency to focus on the problem rather than the solution and on what is wrong rather than what is right with students.

Client factors, which include all of the assets that students bring to the table, are the most potent ingredients in the change process (Bohart & Tallman, 2010). Unfortunately, students' strengths, successes, and other assets are often overlooked. The good news is that client factors are readily available if we just take the time to look and listen for them. This chapter addresses a powerful and overlooked client factor in school solutions—exceptions to the problem. A short definition is provided, followed by strategies for helping students identify and increase exceptions at school.

Definition of Exceptions

Building on exceptions is a hallmark of solution-focused brief therapy (de Shazer et al., 2007). Exceptions refer to situations in which the problem is absent, less frequent, or less intense than usual—minisolutions that are already happening, just not as often as people would prefer.

Returning to Devon in Chapter 1, an exception was discovered when he reported that his math work was more accurate when he was given extra time to complete it. In an effort to build on this exception, Devon's teacher reduced the number of problems on his math sheets and allowed more time for him to complete them.

Benefits of Increasing Exceptions

Many students who display behavior problems are largely unaware of their own strengths, successes, and resources. Their school files include several inches of documentation on their problems and deficiencies. While this information can be helpful in understanding the problem, an exclusive focus on the problem creates a pessimistic attitude about the prospects of change before we even meet the student. Adults and students may become so discouraged by the problem that they are unable to notice non-problems—small successes that may serve as building blocks to larger changes.

For students who are accustomed to hearing more about what they are doing wrong than right, exception-based conversations offer a refreshing change that engages their attention and energy. Exceptions provide factual evidence that students are capable of success, which helps to boost their hope and motivation.

The practical simplicity of increasing exceptions is helpful in working with students of all ages because most students understand and appreciate the commonsense idea of finding something that works and doing more of it. The fact that building on exceptions is easy to understand does not mean that it is easy to do. Old habits are hard to break, and many of us have been trained to respond to problems by diagnosing and analyzing them—in other words, by focusing primarily on the problem and not the exceptions. Exceptions often fall under the radar at first glance, and we need to do some digging to find them. The next section provides techniques for locating exceptions anywhere they can be found.

Strategies for Identifying and Exploring Exceptions

I don't lead musicians, man. They lead me. I listen to them and learn what
they do best.

—Miles Davis, Jazz Musician

The first step in building on exceptions is to find them. The following strategies are
useful in identifying and exploring exceptions.

Listening For Exceptions

Students rarely report exceptions unless they are asked about them. Sometimes,
however, we can pick up hints of exceptions in the student's description of the
problem. The italicized words in the following statements provide clues about
exceptions:

- I am failing *almost* all my classes.
- My parents *rarely* let me do what I want to do.
- I hate everything about school *except* recess and computer time.
- I *usually* forget to do my homework.
- I *hardly ever* get my class work done.

In the first example above, the word "almost" suggests that there is at least one
class that the student is passing. The phrase "hardly ever" in the last example might
prompt us to explore a recent time in which the student has completed the class
work.

Once we discover an exception, we can obtain specific information about related
details and circumstances by asking the following questions:

- What did you do to make it (the exception) happen?
- How was that different from what you've done before?
- Who was around? What did they do?
- What is different about your best class compared to your other classes?

Obtaining details about exceptions is pursued with the same analytic rigor that
is commonly used to explore details of the problem. Both types of information
are useful, but students often show more enthusiasm when discussing exceptions
as compared to problems. In addition to engaging students' attention and hope
by focusing on successes, clarifying the details of exceptions lays the groundwork
for designing exception-based interventions. For example, details about a class in
which the student behaves well can be used to design interventions that incorporate elements of the "exception class" into other classes.

Hints of exceptions can occur at any point during our work with students. In
the following dialogue with a 16-year-old student named Lindsey, the search for
exceptions begins while discussing her goals.

School Practitioner (SP):   What will be the first small sign that things are getting
better here at school?

Lindsey:	I wouldn't have ISS (in-school suspension).
SP:	How often do you have ISS?
Lindsey:	Almost every day. [The word "almost" provides a hint of exceptions.]
SP:	So there have been certain days that you have not had ISS?
Lindsey:	Yes.
SP:	That's interesting. Does it strike you as important that there are some days that you manage to keep yourself out of ISS?
Lindsey:	(Shrugs shoulders.) I guess.
SP:	How important is it for you to stay out of ISS?
Lindsey:	Pretty important. I don't want to be sitting there staring at a wall for an hour while my friends are all hanging out after school. [Once it is clear that she wants to reduce her time in ISS, Lindsey and the practitioner identify and explore times when she did not have ISS.]
SP:	That makes perfect sense. Tell me about a time this month when you went a whole day or more without getting ISS.
Lindsey:	Last week.
SP:	What day?
Lindsey:	I think it was Monday and Tuesday.
SP:	Monday *and* Tuesday. Wow. Two days in a row. How did you do that?
Lindsey:	I don't know. I was having a pretty good time at school.
SP:	A pretty good time?
Lindsey:	Yeah. I don't know what it was. It just happened.
SP:	Hmm. I wonder how you made it happen—what you did differently on the days you didn't have ISS. [The practitioner continued to express curiosity while gathering other details about the exception.]

As illustrated with Lindsey, it is important to listen for subtle hints of exceptions in students' language. Lindsey's comment that she received ISS "almost" every day provided the opportunity to discover and explore exceptions to the ISS problem.

Asking for Exceptions

The following strategies directly elicit exceptions from students:

- When is this problem absent or less noticeable?
- Tell me about a recent time when you did a little better in your science class.
- We've talked about the problem between you and the teacher. I'd also like to learn about the times when things go a little better, even for just a short

time during class. Tell me about one of those times during the last week or so.

■ What is your best class?

■ Tell me about a time in the past few weeks that you made it through the whole day without getting kicked out of class.

Visual displays and drawings can be used to identify exceptions with younger and less verbal students. For example, we can draw three faces on a sheet of paper—one smiling, one neutral, and one frowning—and say, "Some days at school are more like this face (pointing at the frowning face), some days are like this (pointing at the smiling face), and some are in between (pointing at the neutral face). Tell me about a time when school is like this for you (pointing at the smiling face). We can also draw a line across a sheet of paper with occasional spikes while explaining that the flat parts represent problem times and the spikes are times when things are better. Next, we can point to the spikes on the line and say, "Tell me about one of these better times at school." These are just two of the many possible ways that exception-finding questions can be tailored to fit students.

As illustrated next with Jason, age 14, the search for exceptions should never be forced and should always accommodate the student's perspective.

School Practitioner (SP):	When have things been a little better for you in school this week?
Jason:	Never. I get in trouble all the time.
SP:	That must be really hard for you. Which class do you get in trouble a little less in?
Jason:	Probably math class.
SP:	How would you explain that? What is it about math class—or your approach to it—that helps you behave better and get in less trouble?

Instead of challenging Jason's view that things are "never" better at school, the practitioner accepted his perception and rephrased the question in Jason's words to discover the exception. Even when we adjust our language to students, some may prefer not to discuss exceptions. When this occurs, we should honor their preference and talk about something else.

Mining the Miracle Question

The miracle question ("If a miracle happened and this problem suddenly vanished, what would be different at school?") is not only helping in developing goals as discussed in Chapter 8, but in identifying exceptions as well. After students respond to the miracle question, we can discover exceptions by exploring small aspects of the miracle that may have already occurred: "Tell me about one or two pieces of the miracle that have already happened—even just a little—at school."

We can also discover exceptions by exploring specific aspects of the miracle: "Chen, you said that you and Mr. Endres (teacher) would get along better and not argue as much after the miracle. Tell me about a time when you got along better or argued less with Mr. Endres." After Chen describes a couple of peaceful exchanges with Mr. Endres, we can follow up by exploring other details:

- How was that different than other times?
- Who else was around when that happened?
- What was different about your approach to Mr. Endres or his approach to you?

Information from these questions can be used to encourage Chen and Mr. Endres to replicate and increase the conditions associated with exceptions to the classroom problem. Regardless of how small or trivial these aspects of the miracle may seem, they still might serve as building blocks for larger changes.

Using Scaling Questions

In addition to their usefulness in developing goals as noted in Chapter 8, scaling questions are also helpful in identifying exceptions. Consider the following conversation with Macy, an 11-year-old student referred by her teachers for oppositional and disruptive behavior in class.

School Practitioner (SP):	On a scale of 0 to 10 where 10 is the way you want things to be in class and 0 is the worst it could be, where are things right now?
Macy:	3.
SP:	What will you be doing a little differently when it moves to a 4?
Macy:	I don't know.
SP:	Okay. Just take a second to think about a small change at school that might get it to a 3.5 or 4.
Macy:	I guess I would be better in class.
SP:	What would that look like? What would you do different than what you're doing now?
Macy:	I'd like being in class and maybe I'd like my teachers a little better.
SP:	Tell me about a time during the last few days when you've liked class a little more.
Macy:	(Shrugs shoulders.) I don't know.
SP:	What about a time when you liked your teachers better or got along a little better than usual?
Macy:	My science teacher was a little better one day when we were doing group projects in science.
SP:	When was that?
Macy:	Last week when we were working on a project in class.
SP:	How was she better?
Macy:	She helped me glue some things together for the project.

SP:	What was that like for you?
Macy:	It was okay. At least she wasn't yelling at me.
SP:	Yeah. I wonder what it would take to have that kind of thing happen more often, and to make things better between you and your teachers.

The initial scaling question laid the groundwork for identifying exceptions with Macy. In addition to asking what the next higher number would look like—as illustrated with Macy—we can ask if the number was lower at any time during the past few weeks or months. If the student says yes, we can find out what he or she did to contribute to the improvement. This strategy is illustrated in the following conversation with a 12-year-old student named Jacob.

School Practitioner (SP):	On a scale of 0 to 100, where 100 is just the way you want things to be in class and 0 is the worst it could possibly be, where are things right now?
Jacob:	About 20.
SP:	Okay. As you think about the past few months, was there ever a time when the number was lower?
Jacob:	Yes.
SP:	What number was it?
Jacob:	1.
SP:	When was that?
Jacob:	The beginning of the year. I got suspended and they thought I might have to go to court.
SP:	I see. What happened to change the number from 1 at the beginning of the year to a 20?
Jacob:	I don't know.
SP:	It's interesting that it went from 1 to 20 in a couple months. That's 19 whole points. You must be doing something different than you were then when it was a 1.
Jacob:	I'm doing more of the work now. Not all of it. But I wasn't doing any of it when school started.
SP:	What else is different about the "new you" compared to the "old you" when things were a 1 at school?
Jacob:	I don't trash talk the teachers as much as I did.
SP:	Okay. How do you resist the urge to trash talk the teachers when you get mad and feel like doing it?
Jacob:	I just tell myself not to do something and I don't do it.
SP:	Wow. You have that much control over your actions. That's impressive.

As seen with Jacob, using scaling questions to discover "worse times" at school has several advantages. First, it invites students to acknowledge that life is always changing, even when it feels the same from one day to the next. The scaling conversation helped Jacob realize that things have improved at school, a realization that might boost his motivation and hope. Second, a student's description of how things have improved may reveal exceptions and other resources that can be used to build solutions. When asked to explain how the number went from a 1 to a 20, Jacob said that he completed more work (Exception 1) and resisted the urge to trash talk his teachers (Exception 2). Third, scaling questions that explore when things were worse often reveal distinctions between students' previous behavior and current behavior (before/after, old you/new you). These distinctions invite students to consider new and more hopeful stories about themselves and their possibilities.

Discovering Exceptions in Pre-Treatment and Between-Session Changes

Everyone is bound to bear patiently the results of his own example.

—Plato

Pre-treatment change is a special type of exception that refers to improvements in the problem that occur between the scheduling of an appointment and the first meeting with a helper. The first study of pre-treatment change was done in a community mental health agency by a team of solution-focused therapists. They asked clients during the first session if they had noticed any positive changes in their presenting concerns after scheduling their appointment, and two thirds of the clients said yes (Weiner-Davis, de Shazer, & Gingerich, 1987). Subsequent studies have verified that clients often experience relief and improvement just prior to their first session (Mackrill, 2008; Ness & Murphy, 2001).

Some practitioners have observed that merely acknowledging pre-treatment changes can increase people's motivation, self-confidence, and optimism because they realize that they are capable of making improvements on their own (Kindsvater, 2007; O'Hanlon & Weiner-Davis, 2003). Research on pre-treatment change supports the strategy of asking the following questions during the first meeting with students:

■ Sometimes people notice that things get a little better right after they decide to get help or realize that they will be meeting with someone. What have you noticed?
■ Has anything changed for the better since you knew we were going to be meeting?
■ Has anything been different in class since your teacher told you that we would be meeting?

These questions can be modified in the following ways to identify between-session changes—changes that occur between our contacts with students:

■ What's better since we last met?

- What has changed since we talked last week?
- Tell me about something good that happened at school since the last time we met.

As with other types of exceptions, students typically do not report pre-treatment or between-session changes unless they are directly asked about them. Building on pre-treatment and between-session exceptions is like tipping the first domino—one small change provides momentum for another, then another, and so on.

Assigning Observation Tasks

The following observation tasks are helpful in identifying exceptions:

- Between now and next week's meeting, observe anything at school that you want to continue.
- Try to notice the things in your life that you want to continue happening, and make a list so that we can talk about them when we meet next Friday.
- Between now and next Tuesday, observe the things about your approach to school that you would like to continue doing.
- Observe when the problem is not occurring and pay attention to how you are able to make that happen.
- Pay attention to the times you are able to resist the urge to (hit someone, skip school, or whatever the problem is) so that you can help me understand how you do that.

These tasks are particularly helpful for students who feel like "nothing" is right with them or school. None of these tasks challenge or question students' perceptions—they simply invite students to notice the more functional and satisfying aspects of life and school.

As you can see, there are many different ways to identify exceptions. The next section describes strategies for increasing the presence of exceptions at school.

Strategies for Increasing Exceptions

Once an exception is identified, we can encourage students to expand it to other situations and to a greater frequency. Increasing the presence of exceptions at school involves variations of the question, "What would it take to do more of this?"

Increasing Exceptions in Other Situations

The school principal sternly escorted Thomas, age 12, into my office. Thomas was not happy to be there. He stared at the floor as the principal said, "This is Thomas. The teachers and I want you to talk to him." Not a good start.

Thomas and I met a few days later for our first session. When asked about his classes, Thomas indicated a clear preference for science class. He told me "the teacher was cool" and the class was "more interesting" than his other classes. I asked for more details about his science class and how it differed from his other classes. I learned that science was the only class in which Thomas (a) sat close to the teacher and the chalkboard, (b) took notes, (c) occasionally did homework, and (d) arrived to class on time. Thomas and I explored how he might expand one or more of these exception behaviors from science class to his other classes—one class and one behavior at a time. Thomas made a genuine effort to complete more homework and arrive on time in his other classes, which helped him to reduce his discipline referrals by 50 percent during the last two months of the school year. Expanding exceptions to other situations is applicable to any type of exception and to anyone who is connected to the student such as teachers, administrators, parents, siblings, or peers.

Increasing the Frequency of Exceptions

In addition to expanding exceptions to other situations, students and others can be encouraged to increase the frequency of exceptions. Returning to Devon in Chapter 1, we discovered the following exceptions: (a) his math performance was more accurate when he was given more time to complete the problems; (b) he did better on his math homework when his brother Robert helped him with it; and (c) his aunt's affirmations helped him persevere instead of giving up on himself or school. To increase the frequency of these exceptions, Devon's aunt provided more affirmations, Robert helped more often with homework, and his math teacher gave him more time and fewer problems whenever possible. These strategies helped Devon increase the frequency of exceptions by increasing the conditions under which they occurred. Devon's story also illustrates the benefits of including other key people in exception-based interventions.

As illustrated throughout this chapter, *sometimes the best way to resolve a problem is to build on non-problems*—that is, to identify and expand on those times and situations in which the problem is absent or less noticeable. Strategies for identifying and increasing exceptions are summarized in Table 9.1. These strategies and examples of building on exceptions illustrate how large solutions can emerge from small successes. Struggling students typically hear about what is wrong with them or their school performance with little mention of strengths and successes. The power of exception-based interviewing strategies is due in part to the fact that students are more likely to participate in conversations and interventions that acknowledge what is right and what is working for them instead of hearing "more of the same" information about what is wrong and deficient. As one student exclaimed while we were discussing exceptions, "I didn't know I was doing ANYTHING right!"

Summary and Conclusions

Building on exceptions to the problem is based on the practical idea that it is easier to push a river in the direction it is already going than it is to push it in the

TABLE 9.1 Strategies for Identifying and Increasing Exceptions

Strategy	Description	Example
Listening for exceptions	Listening for hints of non-problem situations (exceptions) in students' language	"I have problems with *almost* all of my teachers"
Asking for exceptions	Using exception-finding questions	"When is the problem absent or less noticeable?"
Mining the miracle question	Exploring students' responses to the miracle question to locate exceptions	"What small piece of the miracle is already happening just a little bit?"
Using scaling questions	Asking students what the next number on the scale would look like	"What will you be doing differently when you move from a 3 to a 4?"
Discovering exceptions in pre-treatment and between-session changes	Asking students if they've noticed any changes in the referral problem before the first session or between sessions	"Has anything changed since you found out we were meeting?"; "What has changed since we last met?"
Assigning observation tasks	Inviting students to pay attention to times when the problem is absent or less noticeable at school	"Make a list of things at school that you want to continue happening"
Increasing exceptions in other situations	Inviting students to repeat exception behaviors from one situation (math class) to others (science class)	"How could you do more math class behavior in other classes?"
Increasing the frequency of exceptions	Encouraging students to do "more of" the exception (counting to 5 when frustrated or angry) at school	"What will it take to remember to count to 5 more often at school?"

opposite direction. Exceptions are minisolutions that are already moving in the right direction—and they are there for the asking. This chapter offers several strategies for identifying and increasing exceptions at school. We can identify exceptions by listening for them, asking direct questions, following up on miracle and scaling questions, exploring pre-treatment and between-session changes, and assigning observation tasks. The process of identifying and increasing exceptions is illustrated by examples involving a variety of students and problems. In addition to interviewing students, we can interview teachers and parents, review educational records, and conduct classroom observations with an eye toward discovering exceptions. The theme of resolving school problems by making the most of what works for students is continued in Chapter 10 as we explore other resources that can be applied toward solutions.

Reflection and Application

1. Select a current concern or problem in your life. Now think of an exception to the problem and ask yourself the following questions: What was different about that time? What was different in the way I thought about or responded to the situation? How can I make this happen more often or in other situations? After you've answered the questions, take a minute to reflect on how this process compares to your usual approach to resolving problems.

2. The next time you discuss a problem with a client, friend, or family member, ask him or her to describe times when the problem does not happen or when it is less noticeable. Pick one exception and (a) explore additional details and (b) discuss how the exception might be expanded to a greater frequency or to other situations.

3. To practice the strategy of identifying exceptions through the use of scaling questions, break into pairs and assign one person to the role of the client and the other to the role of the practitioner. After the client describes a concern or problem that they would like to change, the practitioner can ask: (a) On a scale of 0 to 10 where 0 is "the worst it has been," and 10 is "where you want it to be," where would you rate things right now?; (b) What would the next highest number look like?; (c) Tell me about a recent time when this occurred in some form, if only slightly or just a little; and (d) What would it take to make it happen more often?

4. The next time you meet with a student or client for the first time, ask if he or she has noticed any improvements in the problem since scheduling the meeting. If the answer is "yes," then (a) explore the details of these pre-treatment changes and (b) ask what it will take to increase these changes in the future. You can use the same approach to explore between-session changes.

5. Observation tasks can be helpful in identifying exceptions. To practice this strategy, select a current concern or situation that you would like to change and carry out the following steps: (a) Over the next week, observe

and note specific aspects of your approach to this situation that you would like to continue; and (b) ask yourself, "What will it take to increase these things in the future?"

6. What are the major benefits of building on exceptions in working with students to resolve school behavior problems?
7. Describe one small step that you are willing to take in your work with students as a result of the information in this chapter.

ten

Working with What Works

II: Natural Resources

Chapter Objectives

- To highlight the benefits of applying students' natural resources toward school solutions;
- To provide strategies for identifying and applying students' natural resources;
- To describe seven natural resources that can be integrated into school-based interventions.

> Great emergencies and crises show us how much greater our vital resources are than we had supposed.
>
> —William James

> Use what you've got.
>
> —Bob Murphy

Bob Murphy was a practical man who could fix or build just about anything around the house. He rarely made a trip to the hardware store because he preferred to use the tools and materials that were in the garage. More than saving money, he enjoyed the challenge of using what was already available to get the job done. My father and Milton Erickson were a lot alike. Erickson used whatever was available from clients to create customized, one-of-a-kind interventions for each client. He believed that people possessed a wealth of resources regardless of their diagnoses, and his major therapeutic goal was to help them access and apply their own resources. Just as my dad would always find something in the garage to fit the job, Erickson found "something" in each client that could be used to produce change. The pragmatic elegance of Erickson (and my father) fuels this book's belief that students' strengths and resources provide the most efficient path to school solutions.

This chapter describes strategies for identifying and applying the internal and external resources of students. These resources include special interests, talents, values, life experiences, resilience, courage, and solution ideas. Since every student offers a unique set of resources, resource-based interventions are constructed "one student at a time" with no preconceived notions about what they should look like. The integration of student resources into school interventions is supported by a growing body of research on the benefits of incorporating "as much of the client as possible" in the helping process (Bohart & Tallman, 2010; Duncan, 2010; Gassman & Grawe, 2006). You are not likely to find such interventions in lists of evidenced-supported treatments because (a) they cannot be selected or developed before meeting with the student, (b) they are often formulated "on the spot" in collaboration with the student, and (c) they are based completely on material supplied by the student—which is precisely why they work so well.

Benefits of Building on Resources

The benefits of building on resources are similar to those of building on exceptions. Resource-based conversations hold students' attention by emphasizing what is working in their lives instead of what is not working. These conversations convey faith in students' ability to make important changes at school by using qualities and strengths that they already possess. Resource-based interventions also capitalize on the powerful role of client factors in the change process.

Building on resources also enhances the maintenance of students' improvements because these resources are a naturally occurring part of their lives—they were there long before we were and they will be there after we leave. The natural validity of resource-based interventions (a) increases the likelihood that students will continue implementing them after formal services are terminated, and (b) enhances the cultural respect and fit of interventions because they are constructed from existing elements in the student's life.

Identifying and Applying Resources

I am more and more convinced that our great problem is taking advantage of what we've got.

—Thomas Merton

The following strategies are useful in identifying and applying naturally occurring resources in the lives of students. Notice how these strategies—listening, asking, and applying—are similar to those involved in identifying and applying exceptions.

Listening for Resources

Practitioners can pick up on potentially useful resources by being alert to signs of strength, interest, or excitement on the part of the student. I recall my first meeting with Daniel, a 10-year-old student referred for oppositional behaviors—most of which occurred in the afternoons. At one point during the conversation, he said something under his breath that included the word "baseball." When I asked him to repeat it, Daniel said that he would do better in his classes if he was allowed to play baseball at school.

We spent the next few minutes discussing Daniel's love of baseball. He was a serious baseball fan who knew the names, positions, and batting averages of several players on the city's major league baseball team. It was clear from his comments and enthusiasm that baseball was an exciting and important part of his life. We will return to Daniel shortly to illustrate the process of applying students' resources to school solutions.

Asking About Resources

Most students do not volunteer information about their strengths and resources unless they are asked about them. Questions for identifying resources include the following:

- How have you kept things from getting worse?
- How have you handled similar challenges?
- What do you enjoy doing outside of school?
- What would your friends say that you are good at? What do they like the most about you?
- Of all the people in your life, who do you look up to and respect the most? What would he or she advise you to do about this problem?
- Who are the people that help you the most when you have a problem? What is it about them, or about what they do, that is most helpful?
- What do you think might help turn things around at school?

Additional strategies for discovering students' internal and external resources are provided throughout this chapter.

Applying Resources to School Solutions

After we identify students' natural resources, we can explore how one or more of them might be applied to school solutions. In Chapter 1, several resources in Devon's life were incorporated into school-based interventions. These resources included his aunt and older brother, his resilience, and his desire to be the first person in the family to graduate from high school. The fact that the interventions were constructed from naturally occurring resources in Devon's life made it more likely that they would be implemented with integrity and commitment, and that they would continue after formal services ended.

Recall the earlier example of Daniel, the 10-year-old student who loved baseball. After a few minutes of baseball talk, we discussed how the challenges of school were similar to the challenges of baseball. We also talked about how long the base-ball season is and how important it is to not allow a few bad games to ruin the whole season. Daniel agreed to try a baseball approach to his classes. He decided to "step up to the plate" each day and do his best even though he might occasion-ally "strike out" and make mistakes. Things improved over the next couple weeks and his teacher commented on his impressive turnaround. Daniel's intervention emerged from his brief comment about a major interest in his life. As a result, he was able to get behind the intervention and do his best to make it work.

The success of resource-based interventions rests largely on the student's ability to make sense of them and to apply them in personally meaningful ways (Bohart & Tallman, 2010). In addition to engaging students' attention and energy, resource-driven interventions are more culturally sensitive than practitioner-driven inter-ventions that may bear little resemblance to students' everyday lives.

Seven Natural Resources that Promote School Solutions

Since it is impractical to discuss every possible resource that students may offer, I have selected seven resources that are applicable to most students and most problems.

- *Values and beliefs:* Students' deeply held values, beliefs, and world views.
- *Chance events:* Unplanned events in the student's life that enhance solutions.
- *Solution attempts:* Previous attempts to resolve the school problem or similar problems.
- *Resilience:* Ability to withstand and cope with life's challenges, including school problems.
- *Special interests, talents, and hobbies:* Sports, movies, skateboarding, music, mechanical activities, etc.
- *Heroes and influential people:* Parents, siblings, friends, coaches, actors, athletes, musicians, and any other real or fictional heroes to the student.
- *Ideas and opinions:* The student's ideas, opinions, and theories related to school problems and solutions.

The remainder of the chapter describes each of these resources along with strate-gies for applying them to school solutions.

Values and Beliefs

He who has a why to live can bear almost any how.
—Friedrich Nietzsche

Every student has a unique set of values and beliefs that can serve as powerful motivators in building solutions. Sometimes we can pick up on students' values and beliefs by listening to what they say and how they say it. Most of the time, however, we need to ask questions such as the following:

- What do you want your life to stand for?
- What do you value most in your life?
- What is most important to you?
- What kind of life do you want to have 10 or 20 years from now?

Andrea, Age 17

She slowly entered the office, sat down in a chair, and stared at the floor. Andrea, a 17-year-old student referred by her teachers because she had reportedly "shut down and given up on school," had recently mentioned dropping out of school. Andrea was in a special education program for students with cognitive limitations and had done reasonably well up to this point in the school year. When the practitioner told Andrea about her teachers' concerns, she put her face in her hands and quietly sobbed. After a couple minutes of silence, Andrea said, "I can't take it anymore. I'm tired of it." It turns out that she was a frequent target of teasing and cruel comments by some of her peers. Andrea was understandably hurt and frustrated by the steady barrage of insults, and she responded by either yelling obscenities or withdrawing from peers altogether. The withdrawal had become more prevalent in recent weeks. She even slept in some classes to avoid contact with anyone. Dropping out, both mentally and physically, seemed like a good solution to Andrea.

In searching for resources, the practitioner asked Andrea how she had coped with the teasing and other challenges she faced at school. She perked up a little as she described methods that included talking to her best friend, listening to music, and praying. Of all these resources, Andrea became most enthused when she described her belief in God and prayer. The conversation proceeded in the following way.

School Practitioner (SP):	It sounds like your faith in God and prayer is very important to you.
Andrea:	God is always there to watch over me.
SP:	And it helps you to know that God is always there for you?
Andrea:	It helps me a lot.
SP:	How does it help you?
Andrea:	It's just good to know that God is there no matter what.
SP:	So you know that God is there to help you no matter what happens?
Andrea:	Yes.
SP:	You said before that it helps you to pray when things are not going well or when things are bothering you. Have you prayed about the stuff that's been bothering you in school?
Andrea:	(Pauses.) I've prayed some, but I should probably do more.

SP:	I'm not telling you what to do. I was just wondering.
Andrea:	No, I need to pray and ask God to help me. My mom tells me I have to be in school, but it's hard with some of these people.
SP:	It sounds really hard. No wonder you've thought about giving up from time to time. But you haven't given up, which makes me wonder how you've been able to handle this for so long.

The school practitioner and Andrea discussed her strengths and resilience for a few minutes, along with some specific strategies for responding to teasing. Although she did not want to tattle on other students, Andrea agreed to join the practitioner in a conference with her teachers to inform them about the teasing. The following dialogue occurred at the end of the meeting with Andrea.

SP:	We've talked about a lot of things here, Andrea. I've learned a lot about who you are and what helps you hang in there instead of giving up. You're a strong person with a strong faith in God. With everything you've been through, you're still here trying to better yourself and learn as much as you can.
Andrea:	My mom always tells me that I can do anything with God's help. I know God wants me to be the best person I can be. If I learn a lot then maybe I can help other people when I get older.
SP:	You're an amazing person, Andrea. Thanks for meeting with me this morning. If it's okay with you, I'll contact your teachers and we'll set up a time for all of us to meet together like we talked about earlier. How does that sound?
Andrea:	Good.

When Andrea and the practitioner met with her teachers the next day, they assured her that they would address the teasing problem in a manner that would not implicate her as a tattler. Andrea was relieved and visibly moved by their support. Andrea returned a week later to inform the practitioner that one student still teased her, but not nearly as often as before. She went on to say that she prayed hard for the strength to handle things at school, and that she felt better equipped to do so. Her teachers reported that she was more responsive during class and "more like her old self" again.

Andrea's story illustrates how students' values and beliefs can serve as useful resources in addressing school behavior problems. Every student has values that are there for the asking. Helping students to link their school performance and behavior with deeply held values and beliefs can greatly increase their motivation, accountability, and involvement in building solutions.

Chance Events

> Chance is always powerful. Let your hook be always cast. In the pool where you least expect it, will be a fish.
>
> —Ovid

Chance events are a natural part of life. Some unplanned events are stressful and unpleasant while others lead to new insights and solutions.

Mario, Age 6

Mario was referred for services in the hopes of improving his classroom behavior. Most of his problems involved a classmate named Darrell. Previous interventions had focused on helping him resist the urge to respond to Darrell's teasing. Although some improvements occurred, they paled in comparison to the changes that followed a chance event outside of school—an event the school practitioner learned about in the following conversation.

School Practitioner (SP):	Ms. Foster (Mario's teacher) told me things are a lot better here at school. What happened?
Mario:	(Smiles and shrugs shoulders) I don't know. Things just got better.
SP:	They sure did. What did you do to make that happen?
Mario:	Nothing. I just started acting right.
SP:	Ms. Foster told me that you and Darrell are getting along better. Is that true?
Mario:	Yeah, we're friends now.
SP:	Friends? How would you explain that?
Mario:	We're nicer to each other.
SP:	What made you decide to be nicer to Darrell?
Mario:	I don't know. We ride our bikes and play now, that's all.
SP:	Wow. I wonder what happened to make things better.

Mario went on to say that he and Darrell saw each other riding bikes after school the previous week and they rode around the neighborhood together. They did the same thing the next day. Within a week, they considered themselves friends. They even watched cartoons one day after school at Darrell's house.

By definition, we cannot induce or control chance events. We can, however, empower solutions by exploring any such events when they occur. As seen with Mario, one small event led to larger and more permanent changes in his school behavior and in his relationship with Darrell. Success once again resulted from the student's self-styled contribution to a school solution.

Solution Attempts

Most behavior problems occur for weeks or months before a referral is made, so it is useful to find out what has already been done to address the problem. Strategies for exploring solution attempts were presented in Chapter 7, and are addressed briefly here because they represent potentially useful resources. Exploring solution attempts helps students (a) to avoid or discontinue strategies that have not worked, and (b) to consider strategies that have been somewhat successful with the current problem or similar problems. The following questions are useful in exploring solution attempts:

- What have you already tried? How did it work?
- Tell me what you've already done about this problem, and I'll make a list. On a scale of 0 to 10, where 0 is "did not work at all" and 10 is "worked great," how well did each of these things work for you?
- Of all the things you've done, what was most/least helpful?
- What have you thought about trying but haven't tried yet?
- How have you handled similar problems in school? How can you make that work for this problem?

The ongoing experience of a school problem makes it hard for students to stop and think about what has (and has not) worked in addressing the problem. The questions above—and the discussions that follow from them—encourage students to discontinue "more of the same" unsuccessful strategies and to apply previously effective strategies to the current situation.

Resilience

> Adversity has the effect of eliciting talents.
>
> —Horace, Roman poet

When used to describe a physical object, resilience refers to the object's ability to spring back and retain its form after being bent or stretched out of shape. In human terms, resilience is a person's ability to withstand or overcome adverse circumstances. Research in developmental psychology indicates that children have a remarkable ability to overcome challenging circumstances through the use of self-protective and self-righting mechanisms (Brom, Pat-Horenczyk, & Ford, 2009; Henderson, Benard, & Sharp-Light, 2008). In a summary of resilience research, Masten (2001) concluded that resilience is "a common phenomenon" and that "development is robust even in the face of severe adversity" (p. 227).

While some people are more resilient than others, everyone has faced difficult challenges and has demonstrated resilience in one way or another. This changes the question from "if" to "how" students are resilient—and how their resilience could be applied to school solutions. The following questions explore students' resilience:

- How have you kept things from getting worse?
- Why haven't you given up?
- How have you managed to hang in there?

■ Has this problem made you any stronger or wiser? How so? How do you keep your hope alive in a situation like this?

Resilience-based questions convey our faith in the student's ability to cope with the problem, if only to stop it from getting worse or to continue "showing up" instead of giving up altogether. In addition to clarifying specific aspects of students' resilience, the above questions demonstrate respect for their capability and contribution to solutions. Box 10.1 invites you to apply your resilience and resources toward a present challenge in your life.

My most memorable lessons about resilience were taught to me by the students and families I served in one of the most economically depressed communities in the United States. The following story about Carla is one of many such lessons on students' irrepressible ability to bend, but not break, under extremely difficult conditions.

Carla, Age 17

Carla was halfway into her senior year when she was referred for failing two classes and periodically skipping school. Her teachers said that she was academically capable of passing all of her classes and that she could make better grades by applying herself and taking school more seriously.

Carla discussed numerous challenges during the first meeting. Her father moved away when she was an infant. Throughout much of her childhood Carla felt that no one wanted her because she was "a financial burden." She moved between her mother's and uncle's house six separate times and attended eight different schools since kindergarten. Her mother and uncle were investigated several times by social services due to neglect and abuse charges. Carla was currently working 30 hours a week at a restaurant to support herself and her mother. She often worked from

---

Box 10.1 Applying Your Resilience and Resources

Think about a previous situation in your life that was so difficult that you wondered if you would survive it. But you did. Somehow you managed to get through it and keep walking.

1. How did you do it?
2. What internal or external resources helped you get through it?
3. How could you apply one or more of these resources to a current challenge or goal in your life?
4. Based on your answers to these questions, list one small step that you are willing to take next week to address your current challenge or goal.

The same sequence of questions can be used with students and others to acknowledge their resilience-based resources and encourage them to apply these resources to school solutions.

midnight to morning and went directly to school after her shift. The following exchange took place at the start of our second meeting.

School Practitioner (SP):	I've thought about our meeting last week, and I have a question for you. With all the hardships you've had to deal with in your life, how have you resisted the temptation to give up on school altogether and just quit?
Carla:	Why would I do that? I've got everything ahead of me and I'm in my senior year. I've made it this far and I'm sure not stopping now.
SP:	Sounds like you have a lot to look forward to.
Carla:	I do. I mean, I'm sure I'll have problems. Everybody does. But I've had it worse than a lot of kids, so I know something about how to handle problems.
SP:	I know you do.
Carla:	I almost gave up two or three years ago. I wanted to quit school and live somewhere else. But I stayed and I'm glad I did.
SP:	What's different about the new Carla compared to the old Carla?

She described differences between the new Carla and old Carla, including her growing determination to make something of her life. Various aspects of her resilient approach to life were incorporated into practical interventions for improving her school attendance and grades. These interventions were designed in collaboration with Carla and included: (a) using self-talk strategies to remind herself how difficult it has been to get this far in school and how important it is to "stay at it" through the second half of the school year; (b) approaching her boss about adding hours on different days and not working all night on Thursdays because most of her tests were on Friday; and (c) asking her teachers if she could occasionally tutor younger students in science because she was interested in becoming a teacher and science was one of her strongest subjects.

Carla enjoyed the opportunity to discuss "what was right" with her and to build on her personal strengths and assets. Despite continued difficulties at home and school, Carla passed all of her classes, graduated in May, and made plans to attend a local community college.

Exploring the resilience of students does not minimize the seriousness or impact of problems such as child abuse, inadequate housing, and unmet nutritional needs. In the midst of these challenges, students are always doing something to survive and cope. In other words, they are being resilient. Helping students to recognize and apply their resilience is a key aim of student-driven interviewing.

Special Interests, Talents, and Hobbies

"You can't rearrange furniture unless you're invited into the house" is one of my favorite metaphors because it addresses the all-important issue of establishing strong relationships with students by engaging their attention and involvement.

Many students enter services as involuntary clients because they are referred by their parents or teachers. One way to bond with students and engage their attention is to talk about something that is meaningful to them—such as special interests or hobbies—and to explore connections between these resources and school solutions.

Every student has unique interests, hobbies, and talents that can be explored through the following types of questions:

- What do you enjoy doing outside of school?
- What excites you the most in life?
- What is it about your hobby that makes it fun and worthwhile for you?
- How would you or other people finish this sentence about you: "Mary is really good at …"?
- If you could do anything you wanted, what would it be?

Daniel, Age 10 (Revisited)

Incorporating hobbies and special interests into school-related interviews was illustrated earlier with Daniel, the student who loved baseball. After discovering Daniel's passion for baseball, we explored connections between the challenges of baseball and the challenges of school. Daniel's love of baseball resulted in a school intervention framed in baseball language and metaphors such as getting a hit, striking out, pitching a full game, making occasional errors, and playing hard until the last out. Presenting the intervention in Daniel's language helped to sustain his attention and involvement throughout the change process.

Every student is interested in *something*. Our task is to discover what it is and how it might be incorporated into school interventions.

Heroes and Influential People

We all need someone we can lean on.

—The Rolling Stones

Helping people to identify and enlist support from key people in their lives has been shown to improve therapy outcomes (Gassman & Grawe, 2006; Harmon et al., 2007). Most students have heroes and influential people in their lives who may serve as valuable resources in resolving problems. Heroes and influential people can include family members, friends, neighbors, mentors, musicians, actors, writers, and fictional characters in books, movies, or cartoons. The common element of all such people is their ability to inspire and influence students.

The following questions help to identify key figures in the student's life and to explore the nature of their influence:

- Who are your biggest heroes?
- Of all the people in your life, who do you respect the most? Why do you respect this person so much?
- Which of your teachers do you get along with best at school?

- Of everyone you have known in your life, who would be most surprised that you're having this problem? Why would this person be surprised? What does he or she know about you that others don't?
- If you could put together a team of people to help you with this problem, who would be on the team?

Heroes and respected people can be employed in a number of creative ways to encourage a different response to the school problem. They can be invited to attend school meetings or be contacted by phone during the interview. We can also encourage students to contact them for input and advice. The following questions help students link the ideas and advice of key people to potential school solutions:

- What would (hero/influential person) do about this situation?
- What do you think (hero's name) might advise you to do?
- If your grandmother was sitting here, what would she tell you to do?
- If you followed your hero's advice, would it make things better at school? (If yes) What small part of that advice are you willing to act on next week?
- How do you go about getting help from the people you respect most? How willing are you to do that now?

Enlisting the influence of heroes and respected people in the student's life is more efficient and respectful than relying solely on our influence or attempting to build new resources from scratch. Heroes and key people are there for the asking, and most of them are willing to do whatever they can to help the student.

Ideas and Opinions

> People are generally better persuaded by the reasons which they have themselves discovered than by those which have come into the minds of others.
>
> —Blaise Pascal

The ideas and opinions of those who are closest to the school problem—students, teachers, and parents—comprise one of the most underrated resources of all. Unfortunately, the input of students is often excluded from the helping process despite their firsthand experience of the problem. The following strategies help to elicit students' ideas and opinions about possible solutions:

- What do you think might help turn things around?
- I've heard other people's ideas, but I want to know what *you* think would help improve things at school.
- Since you know more about this than I ever will, I'd appreciate hearing your ideas about what needs to happen to make things better at school.
- What is your theory about the problem and solution?

Students who display behavior problems are rarely asked for their ideas about anything, much less about possible solutions. They seldom occupy the role of helper or advisor because they are always the ones being helped and advised. As a result, they begin to view themselves as passive participants in an adults-only version of school intervention. The following questions cast students in the role of advisors by tapping their firsthand experience with the problem and potential solutions:

- If you were the counselor, what advice would you give to a student who is struggling with this type of problem?
- I appreciate your willingness to help other students and me by sharing what you've learned about paying attention. What would you say to other third graders who ask what they can do to pay better attention in class?
- What can I say to someone who says, "Why should I pay attention in class when I can have more fun playing around?"
- Pretend you are the teacher and you're teaching a class called, "How to Stand Up to Problems Instead of Letting Them Push You Around." What would you teach the students in this class?
- Based on your knowledge of Mr. Badmouth (the student's name for the problem) and the tricks he uses to get students into trouble, what would you suggest to others who want to take control of their school life instead of letting Mr. Badmouth push them around?

When placed in the role of an expert advisor to others, students often develop new insights and increased accountability regarding their own school performance. It is not unusual for students to say, "I need to take my own advice," after hearing themselves offer advice to others.

I am amazed at how often students provide valuable intervention material if only they are asked. We have much to gain and nothing to lose by requesting their opinions and solution ideas. Even when students say "I don't know" or when their ideas are unsuccessful, inviting their input in this way strengthens the alliance and conveys our respect for their wisdom and experience.

Table 10.1 summarizes each of the natural resources in this chapter along with examples of how to apply them to school solutions.

Summary and Conclusions

Every student has valuable "natural resources" that can be applied toward school solutions. This chapter describes practical strategies for building solutions from a wide variety of naturally occurring resources in the lives of students. Identifying and applying students' resources extends the book's theme of building solutions from "what is right" and "what is working" for students instead of focusing on what is wrong or missing.

Common resources include values, chance events, solution attempts, resilience, special interests, personal heroes, and solution ideas. Integrating these resources into school interventions enhances outcomes by engaging students' attention and involvement in the change process. Behavioral improvements that are prompted by resource-based interventions are likely to be maintained because they are based on natural elements of the student's life—elements that were there before we

TABLE 10.1 Description and Application of Students' Natural Resources

Resource	Description	Application
Values/beliefs	Students' deeply held values ("big values"), beliefs, and world views	Help students link school performance to their "big values"
Chance events	Unplanned events in the student's life that enhance solutions	Be alert to chance events and explore their influence on school problems and solutions
Solution attempts	Previous attempts to resolve the current problem or similar problems	Help students to avoid "more of the same" ineffective strategies; identify and modify strategies that have been somewhat effective with this problem or similar problems
Resilience	Ability to cope with and survive life's challenges, including school problems	Ask students how they have coped with school problems and kept things from getting worse
Special talents, interests, and hobbies	Sports, music, movies, skateboarding, mechanical activities, etc.	Explore connections between students' special interests and solutions to the school problem
Heroes and influential people	Relatives, friends, and others figures (real or fictional, living or deceased) who students respect and admire	Ask students how their heroes might respond to the problem, or what advice they would offer
Ideas and opinions	Student's ideas and opinions related to solutions to the problem	Ask students what they think might help improve things at school, or what advice they have for other students struggling with similar problems

arrived and will remain there after we leave. The next and final chapter addresses the topic of empowering progress whenever it occurs in our work with students.

Reflection and Application

1. What are the major benefits of applying students' natural resources toward school solutions?

2. Pair up with a partner and describe a few internal and external resources that have helped you handle a significant challenge in your life. It is not necessary to share any information about the challenge itself, just the resources that helped you get through it. Switch roles and repeat the exercise.

3. If someone asked you about your special skills and talents, what would you say? What would your friends or coworkers say? How can these skills and talents be applied to your work with students?

4. Box 10.1 displays a sequence of questions aimed at helping people acknowledge and apply their inherent resilience and resources. To practice hosting resilience-based conversations, pair up and ask your partner to think of a current challenge or goal. Next, ask your partner to think of a personal example of resilience and to respond to the following questions: (a) How did you manage to get through it?; (b) What specific resources—within or outside of yourself—were most helpful?; (c) Of all those resources, which ones could help you with your current challenge or goal?; and (d) How could you apply this resource in some small way during the next week?

5. Think about a student with whom you are currently working (or have worked with in the past) and consider how his or her special interests or hobbies might be (or might have been) applied toward a school solution.

6. Think about a current problem or goal in your life. If you could consult with a couple of your personal heroes, what advice would they offer? Does this seem like good advice for your present situation? If so, list one or two specific ways that you could put their advice into action during the next week.

7. Describe one small step that you are willing to take in your work with students as a result of the information in this chapter.

eleven

Keeping the Ball Rolling in the Right Direction

Chapter Objectives

- To highlight the importance of "keeping the ball rolling" by empowering students' progress whenever it occurs;
- To describe six strategies for empowering desired changes;
- To illustrate strategies for empowering progress with a variety of students.

> To become what we are capable of becoming is the only end of life.
> —Baruch Spinoza

One of my practicum assignments during graduate school was to work with Angela, a high school student described by her teachers as unmotivated and oppositional. Neither Angela nor her teachers reported any progress after our first few meetings. Then something happened for which I was not prepared—things got better! Yikes, I thought, now what do I do? As Angela described several positive changes at school, I responded with mundane statements such as "nice job" and "that's really great"—not exactly words of great inspiration or empowerment. I was so intent on getting the ball rolling that I did not know what to do once it started moving in the right direction.

I now realize that my struggle to respond effectively to Angela's progress is a common one for trainees and practitioners. Most of the research and literature on school-based intervention focuses on getting change started with minimal attention to keeping it going. Helping people initiate change will (and should) continue to be a major focus of training programs in the helping professions. But we also need to know how to help students like Angela maintain desired changes— that is, to keep the ball rolling in the right direction at school. This chapter describes practical strategies for doing so in conversations with students. But first, I want to briefly discuss the interplay between monitoring and empowering progress in student-driven interviewing.

The Interplay Between Monitoring and Empowering Progress

The first step in empowering desired changes is to notice when they occur—which requires us to closely monitor progress throughout our work with students. For starters, we can monitor progress by listening closely for any hints of change in students' comments during the conversation. We can also obtain students' feedback on formal rating scales, such as the Outcome Rating Scale, or informal scaling questions ("On a scale of 1 to 10, with 1 being 'the worst it can be' and 10 'the best it can be,' how would you rate the school problem/goal during the past week?"). Chapter 4 describes these methods more thoroughly, but they are mentioned here to emphasize the ongoing interplay between monitoring and empowering progress as illustrated in Figure 11.1.

Techniques for empowering progress can be used as soon as we meet students and continue throughout the helping process. When they report no progress, we can explore what can be done differently to promote change. When students report *any* improvements, no matter how small, we can encourage them to build on these changes by using one or more of the strategies that follow.

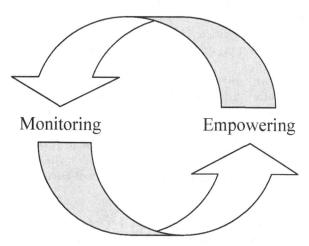

Monitoring   Empowering

FIGURE 11.1   Interplay Between Monitoring and Empowering Progress

Strategies for Keeping the Ball Rolling in the Right Direction

Those who are lifting the world upward and onward are those who encourage more than criticize.

—Elizabeth Harrison

The remainder of the chapter describes six interviewing strategies that help students keep the ball rolling in the right direction when things start improving at school. Many of these strategies are applicable to teachers, parents, and others involved in the change process.

Giving Credit

Giving credit to students begins with the belief that they are the true heroes of the change process. Many students do not automatically assume credit for positive changes at school. Some view progress as a fluke or stroke of luck, while others attribute it to external factors such as the start of medication or counseling.

Regardless of whether counseling or medication has just begun, it is the student who completes more work or behaves better in class—not the intervention. The student makes the intervention work, not the other way around. Without minimizing the impact of practitioners or their methods, the ultimate credit for successful change belongs to students. Therefore, it is important that they view desired changes as resulting from something *they* did—and something they can repeat in the future. The following questions give credit to students by exploring how they made positive changes at school:

- How did you do it?
- What made you decide that now was the time for action?
- How did you know to do that?
- Some students take medication and it doesn't work. How did you make it work for you?
- What are you doing differently to make things better at school?
- How did you resist the urge to do what you used to do?

These questions clarify students' role in school improvements and invite them to take credit for positive changes. Connecting improvements to students' decisions and actions increases their confidence and self-efficacy. Self-efficacy—the belief in one's ability to solve problems and achieve goals—helps students handle setbacks and maintain progress (Lippke, Wiedemann, Ziegelmann, Reuter, & Schwarzer, 2009; Margolis & McCabe, 2006; Molden & Dweck, 2006). The following examples illustrate the strategy of giving students credit for school-related improvements.

Greg, Age 12

Greg was referred by his sixth-grade math teacher for attention problems, behavior problems, and failure to complete homework. He had recently begun taking medication (Cylert) to improve his attention at school. The following conversation occurred in response to Greg's self-reported increase from 3.3 to 5.4 on the school scale of the Child Outcome Rating Scale (CORS). Earlier in the day, his teacher reported similar changes on the CORS and commented that his class behavior and homework had improved greatly during the previous week.

In the next excerpt, the school practitioner attempts to clarify Greg's role in recent improvements. He initially attributes the changes to his mother and his new medication. The practitioner accepts Greg's view while inviting him to take credit for his contributions.

School Practitioner (SP):	Wow, Greg. Your mark on the school scale went from 3.3 to 5.4. That's a big jump. How did you do it?
Greg:	I'm getting more work done and doing my homework right after school.
SP:	That's a pretty big change from before, isn't it?
Greg:	(Nods "yes.") I used to play around more in class, and I would do homework—well, *if* I did homework—I would do it after supper when it got dark outside.
SP:	Okay. So you're doing more work at school, and you changed your homework time. How did you do that?
Greg:	Well, I started taking these pills that help me concentrate and get my work done. And my mom kind of changed the homework time for me (laughs). I get it done and then I can go outside.
SP:	I see. So you're taking these pills and your mom helped you change your homework schedule, and those things are working out pretty good.
Greg:	Yes.
SP:	That's good. I'm wondering how you made the pills and the new homework time work. [Even when success is attributed to outside factors such as medication or intervention by others, we can still explore the student's role in making these strategies work.]
Greg:	What do you mean?
SP:	Well, I know some kids who take medication, but it doesn't work. What did you do to make it work for you?
Greg:	(Shrugs shoulders.) I don't know, I guess I just figured it was time to start doing work. [Later in the conversation ...]
SP:	When we talked about this a couple weeks ago, you told me how hard it was to do homework when it was light outside and your friends were out playing. Remember that?
Greg:	Yeah.

SP:	Is it still hard to do work in class and to do homework when it's light outside?
Greg:	Sometimes.
SP:	I'll bet it is. But somehow the temptation to push schoolwork and homework aside doesn't have the hold on you that it used to. How do you resist the urge to play around in class or to go outside right after school like you used to?
Greg:	I just decided it's not worth getting F's in spelling and math. I don't want to flunk out of school like a lot of people do. I want to graduate.
SP:	It's still tempting, right?
Greg:	A little, I guess, but I usually get homework done pretty quickly, so I can still get outside by about four thirty or something. Plus I don't get yelled at by my mom.

The practitioner continued to give Greg credit as they explored other ways to sustain improvements and resist old habits. Even when students attribute progress to factors outside themselves—as illustrated with Greg—we can invite them to take credit for their unique role and contributions to school improvements.

Damika, Age 7

Damika was referred by her teacher (Ms. Hammill) due to academic and behavioral problems at school. This excerpt was taken from the opening moments of the meeting with Damika following recent improvements in her school performance.

School Practitioner (SP):	Damika, Ms. Hammill tells me that you've really improved. She said that your behavior is better and your grades are better, especially in math. What are you doing differently to make all this happen?
Damika:	Well, I don't talk as much as I used to, unless we're playing. I stopped falling asleep in class and I stopped getting up and walking around when the teacher was talking.
SP:	That's a lot of stuff.
Damika:	(Nods "yes" and smiles.)
SP:	When you say you don't talk as much unless you're playing, what does that mean?
Damika:	Well, you're not supposed to talk in class, but we're allowed to talk at recess on the playground, and sometimes she lets us talk in class.
SP:	Okay. So does that mean you're talking when you're allowed to, and you're not talking as much when you're not allowed to?
Damika:	Yes.

SP:	In the past, you would talk when you weren't supposed to, like during class when the teacher was talking or when you were supposed to be working on something instead of talking.
Damika:	That's why I got in more trouble and I got lower grades.
SP:	Okay. Let me see if I understand this. In the past when you did those things more, you got in more trouble and you got lower grades. Is there a different way you approach your schoolwork now, like in reading and math? [Unless students are given the chance to reflect on their role in bringing about positive changes, they may view progress as a fluke without considering their contributions.]
Damika:	Well, we had to do our math packet. That was half of our grade. If you didn't turn it in you got an F. So I did my packet, and I did all my schoolwork and homework. And that got me a B.

We will resume the conversation with Damika in the next section. As illustrated with Greg and Damika, students respond well to receiving credit because it portrays them as key players in the change process. Teachers and parents can be given credit in similar ways following positive changes in students' school performance.

Exploring the Personal and Social Effects of Improvements

Discussing the personal and social impact of desired changes also helps to empower progress. Positive changes at school can enhance students' self-image, motivation, and relationships with teachers and parents. The following questions are useful in exploring the personal and social consequences of school improvements:

- What have these changes taught you about yourself?
- What effect has this had on your overall attitude and approach toward school?
- How is the "new you" different than the "old you"?
- How do your teachers and parents treat you differently now that you've made these changes?
- How would your teachers describe your approach to school now as compared to two months ago?
- What other changes have you noticed since you started coming to school more often?

These strategies invite students to reflect on specific effects of progress that they may not have considered. We now pick up with Damika where the previous conversation left off. The following exchange occurred right after Damika said that she had completed her math packet and improved her grade from an F to a B.

SP:	Are you telling me you went from an F to a B in math?
Damika:	(Smiles and nods "yes.") I did.
SP:	Wow, that's a big change. How did it feel to bring your grade up like that?
Damika:	It felt great.
SP:	Did it prove something about you?
Damika:	Yeah. It proved I could do it. See, I never really cared about how I did in school. If I got a low grade, I just said "I don't care." It didn't bother me.
SP:	Would it bother you now?
Damika:	(Nods "yes.") I don't want to get low grades anymore.
SP:	So your attitude about grades has changed?
Damika:	Yes.
SP:	Does the "new you" care more about grades than the "old you"?
Damika:	A lot more.
SP:	What else is different about the "new you" than the "old you"? [This discussion invites Damika to consider the personal impact of positive changes on her self-perceptions and attitudes toward school. The following exchange, which occurred a few minutes later, explores the social effects of her recent improvements.]
SP:	Did anybody else react to this change?
Damika:	Yeah, my mom and my dad.
SP:	How did they respond?
Damika:	They gave me money and took me out to eat.
SP:	Wow. So not only did it give you a better feeling about yourself, but it also led to some pretty cool stuff with your parents.
Damika:	They said they were very proud of me.
SP:	And how did that feel for you?
Damika:	It was nice. Because we used to argue about school, and now we don't.
SP:	That's great. What about Ms. Hammill (Damika's teacher)? Does she treat you any differently now?
Damika:	Yes. She's a lot nicer.
SP:	How is she nicer?
Damika:	When I had bad grades, she didn't really help me because I really didn't want to do the work. But now she helps me and she's a lot nicer.
SP:	That's great, Damika. What else is different at home or school?
Damika:	I used to get detention or have to stay in from recess, and I don't have to do that anymore. One day I did, but I used to have to stay in almost every day at the beginning of the year.

We will return to the final segment of the conversation with Damika shortly. As seen above, exploring the personal and social effects of positive changes helps to empower progress by inviting students to reflect on and describe the ripple effects of school improvements.

Enlisting Students as Consultants

Enlisting students as consultants involves asking them for advice in helping others who are struggling with similar problems. When students are asked for their advice, it empowers progress by reminding them of what they did to improve their schoolwork or behavior.

To enlist students as consultants, I often tell them that my job is to help others with struggles that are similar to the ones they are facing or have faced in the past. Next, I ask them to share any tips and advice they have for other students based on their wisdom and experiences. In the next excerpt from the end of the interview with Damika, the practitioner requests her advice for other students.

School Practitioner (SP):	I need your help with something, Damika. My job is to help students change so that school goes better for them. I meet a lot of students who are struggling in school just like you were. When I meet people like you who have made important changes, I try to learn as much as I can about how they did it so that I can help other students. Since you're an expert now on improving things at school, I want to learn as much as I can from you. Will you help me?
Damika:	(Nods "yes" and smiles.) [Like most students, Damika was pleased to be treated as a respected consultant and very willing to share her wisdom with others.]
SP:	Okay, let's say a third-grade student came up to you and said, "Damika, I want to get better grades and do better in school. How can I do that?" What would you say to that student?
Damika:	I would say, "You need to pay attention to the teachers or substitute teacher. Don't throw spitballs or pencils or erasers. And don't get an attitude."
SP:	What kind of attitude do you need to get good grades?
Damika:	You need to have a good attitude and not a bad attitude.
SP:	How can you tell that someone has a good attitude?
Damika:	They're happy and they smile a lot. When you're acting happy and someone gets mad at you, like when they try to hit you and stuff, you don't hit back. You just walk away.
SP:	How does someone with a good attitude approach their schoolwork, like in math and reading?
Damika:	They don't pay attention to the people who are trying to get them in trouble.
SP:	What are some other ideas you have for this student?

Damika:	I'd tell her, "Don't pay attention to kids who are trying to get you in trouble." And I'd tell her to do all her homework and schoolwork. Raise your hand and ask questions if you don't know what the teacher is talking about so you can stay on the same subject. Volunteer more and answer questions in class. And whatever you do, don't try to be a teacher's pet, because it will probably annoy them.

Enlisting students as consultants is one of my favorite ways to empower progress because referred students are seldom asked for their opinions about anything, much less for their expert advice to me and other students. As seen with Damika, most students enjoy the rare opportunity to share their wisdom from the position of a helper rather than the one being helped.

In addition to obtaining students' suggestions during interviews, we can ask them to dictate or write up their story as part of our ongoing collection of "success stories" that can be shared with other students. The request can range from general ("Write a story about how you made these changes") to specific ("Make a list of things that third-grade students should do to pay better attention in class"). I have also invited students to become members of my Helper Club (elementary) or Consultant Club (secondary), consisting of students who have improved their school performance and granted me permission to contact them in the future for ideas and advice (Murphy, 2008). The fact that no student has ever declined the invitation to join the club attests to students' favorable response to being treated as capable advisors and consultants. Box 11.1 displays a Consultant Club certificate.

Exploring Students' Intentions to Maintain Progress

> Let the good times roll.
> —Ric Ocasek, The Cars

Exploring students' intentions to maintain progress is another way to keep the ball rolling in the right direction once it starts. The following questions help students clarify their intentions and plans to sustain progress:

Box 11.1 Consultant Club Certificate

This is to recognize
Lisa Smith
as an
official member of the Consultant Club.
The Consultant Club consists of students who have made important
changes and are willing to consult with Dr. Murphy to help others.
_____ , Consultant
_____ , Dr. Murphy, Club President

- Do you plan to continue these changes?
- What needs to happen for these improvements to continue?
- What can you do to keep things moving in the right direction?
- How are you going to stick with this plan in the future?

We can also use social relationship questions to explore what others might suggest to help the student maintain progress:

- What would your teacher say needs to happen for these changes to continue?
- If you asked your older sister what you could do to keep things moving in the right direction at school, what do you think she would say?
- Think of two people that you respect a lot. What would they advise you to do to stay on track at school?

The above questions invite a variety of ideas that the student might not otherwise consider.

Angelique, Age 16

The following excerpt is taken from a conversation with Angelique, a tenth grader referred for truancy, talking out in class, and refusing to serve detention. The meeting took place after two consecutive days during which Angelique received no discipline slips. After giving her credit for arriving to school on time and behaving better, the practitioner asks Angelique about her intentions to maintain her recent improvements.

School Practitioner (SP):	So you set your alarm and reminded your mother to wake you if you weren't up by 7:30. Did the alarm go off?
Angelique:	Yes. And I got up.
SP:	Wow. I know some college students and other adults who struggle with getting up by an alarm. They keep hitting the snooze button and end up being late for school or work. What's your secret?
Angelique:	(Laughs.) I put it all the way across the room so I have to get up to shut it off.
SP:	What a great idea!
Angelique:	Yeah, my mom was pretty surprised.
SP:	Surprised?
Angelique:	About me getting up on time and going to school.
SP:	Have you ever done that before without reminders or somebody else waking you?
Angelique:	Sometimes, but not too much.
SP:	What made you decide to do it now?
Angelique:	They told me I could end up in court or jail for not going to school. I don't really believe them. My friend didn't go to school for a long time and they didn't do anything to her.

SP:	They didn't do anything?
Angelique:	Well, they called her house and threatened to take her to court. But they never did.
SP:	Interesting. Are you planning to come to school more now or not? [Asking instead of assuming keeps the ball in Angelique's court and gives her the chance to state her intentions in her own words.]
Angelique:	More.
SP:	That sounds like hard work. How are you going to stick with your plan to come to school more when you're really tired and don't feel like getting up?
Angelique:	I'm just going to do what I'm doing now. Set my alarm and just get up in the morning. That's the biggest problem, getting up in the morning. I like to stay up late.
SP:	Yes. I remember you saying you stayed up until three or four in the morning sometimes. Have you done that these last couple of nights before coming to school?
Angelique:	One night I was up until two in the morning. But the other night I went to sleep about midnight.
SP:	If your mom was here, what would she say needs to happen for you to get up and get to school on time?
Angelique:	She'd probably say to just keep setting the alarm. That saves her from trying to wake me up.
SP:	What else would she say would help you get up and get to school on time?
Angelique:	Go to bed earlier. She's always telling me that.
SP:	So how are you planning to handle the sleep thing?
Angelique:	I might just try to go to bed at 11 a couple nights a week. I don't know if I can go to sleep that early.
SP:	I don't know. I guess you can try it and see what happens.

This conversation provided the opportunity for Angelique to describe and refine her plans to keep the ball rolling in the right direction. Like other strategies for empowering progress, this one capitalizes on the idea that people who explicitly state their behavioral plans are more likely to follow through on them (Van Houten, Van Houten, & Louis Malenfant, 2007).

Preparing for Setbacks

The way I see it, if you want the rainbow, you gotta put up with the rain.
—Dolly Parton

Although students are naturally encouraged by their progress, they may also fear that it won't last. Positive changes may be accompanied by apprehensive thoughts such as, "What if I have a really bad day?" or "I hope I don't mess this up." Preparing students for the inevitable bumps and setbacks along the road to improvement enhances their ability to cope with them when they occur. Helping students prepare for setbacks involves (a) explaining that setbacks are a normal part of the change process and (b) developing strategies for handling setbacks when they occur. The following examples incorporate both of these elements:

- Most of the time, important changes do not happen in a straight line. It's more like two steps forward, one step back, and so on. What can you do if you notice that you're having a bad day at school?
- What can you do if you start having a little more trouble with one of your teachers again?
- Everybody has a bad day now and then, even after things start getting better. Maybe we can kick around some ideas for how you could handle those times when things might not go as well as they're going now.

Seth, Age 11

The following conversation illustrates the strategy of preparing for setbacks with Seth, a fifth grader who improved his classroom behavior. The dialogue picks up after Seth had described two strategies that helped him behave better in class—arriving to class on time and ignoring his friend (Ashley) when she tried to get him to "talk about other stuff" instead of paying attention and doing class work.

School Practitioner (SP):	These changes seem to be working pretty well.
Seth:	(Nods "yes.") As long as I can keep doing it.
SP:	Do you think you'll be able to do that?
Seth:	I hope so.
SP:	I know it's important to you to have the freedom that we talked about instead of getting into trouble like you used to, having to stay after school, and getting grounded at home and all that.
Seth:	Definitely. This is better. I just hope I can keep it up. I was late a couple days ago and I got in trouble again. [Like most people who make important changes, Seth was understandably apprehensive about his ability to sustain progress. Next, the practitioner compliments Seth on the changes he has made and inquires about how he might prepare for occasional setbacks.]
SP:	It takes hard work to make the kind of changes you've made. It says a lot about your strength and courage, because changes like this are not easy. One thing I've learned from people who make important changes like you've made is that there are usually some bumps and slips along the way. You know, things might go well for a few days, then there's a bad day, then a good again, and so on. (The practitioner draws a

line with peaks and dips on a sheet of paper.) This is the way important changes usually go, and these slips (pointing to dips in the line) are a normal part of it. Like the other day when you got in trouble in math class, that's one of these times (pointing to the dip in the line). It's a normal part of making changes like you've made. The important thing is how we handle these setbacks when they happen. Does that make sense?

Seth:	Yes.
SP:	So let's say you're in class some day and you and Ashley start talking and you end up get in trouble. How will you handle that?

Seth and the practitioner developed the following strategies that he could use to handle setbacks: (a) reminding himself that setbacks are a normal part of change; (b) focusing on his goal of passing to sixth grade; (c) apologizing to the teacher; and (d) explaining to Ashley that if she wants to be his friend, then she needs to respect his goal of doing better in class. As illustrated with Seth, explicitly discussing setbacks encourages students to develop effective strategies for responding to them when they occur.

Offering Follow-up Services

When goals are reached and formal contact with students is discontinued, we can offer follow-up services to help them maintain their improvements. Follow-up services should be presented in an invitational manner rather than being forced on students. This might involve offering monthly booster sessions throughout the school year to assess progress and make adjustments as needed. The experience of simply meeting again can reinforce previous conversations and remind students of strategies aimed at empowering progress.

Chris, Age 17

The next exchange demonstrates the strategy of offering follow-up services to Chris, a high school student who had made solid improvements in school behavior over the past few weeks. Chris and the practitioner have agreed to discontinue weekly meetings because things are on track and going well at school. The dialogue begins with Chris thanking the practitioner.

Chris:	Thanks for your help. I was worried there for a while.
School Practitioner (SP):	I was too, but I was really impressed with your ability to hang in there. Some people would have given up long ago, but you stayed with it and made it happen.
Chris:	I'm just glad it worked.
SP:	Me too. I know we talked about not meeting every

	week, but that doesn't mean we can't ever meet again. I'd like to check in with you now and then to see how things are going if that's okay.
Chris:	That's fine.
SP:	I don't want to keep you out of class a long time, but maybe we could meet next month to see how things are going at school.
Chris:	Sounds good.
SP:	If you want to meet before then for any reason, just let me know and we'll do it. Okay?
Chris:	Okay.

Although it is best if we conduct follow-up meetings ourselves given our relationship and history with the student, some work schedules and circumstances may prevent us from doing so. If it is not possible to meet directly with the student, we can (a) maintain contact by phone, e-mail, or other such methods, or (b) have another person check in periodically with the student to monitor and empower progress.

One sure thing about life is that it always changes. The fact that students are behaving successfully when we end formal services offers no guarantee about how things will go in the weeks to come. Offering follow-up services ensures students that our door is always open for future contact as needed.

Table 11.1 summarizes strategies for empowering students' progress and keeping the ball rolling in the right direction at the first sign of improvement.

Summary and Conclusions

Training programs place so much emphasis on getting change started that it is easy to underestimate the importance of keeping the change going once people make improvements. This chapter describes six practical strategies for empowering progress and keeping the ball rolling in the right direction when students make improvements at school—giving students credit by attributing positive changes to their efforts and choices, exploring the personal and social benefits of progress, enlisting students as consultants by asking their advice for other students who experience similar problems, exploring students' intentions to maintain progress, helping students prepare for setbacks, and offering follow-up contacts to help students maintain improvements after formal services end. These strategies can be used alone or in combination with each other to help students keep the ball rolling in the right direction once they start making positive changes at school.

Reflection and Application

1. Describe the interrelationship between monitoring and empowering progress.

TABLE 11.1 Strategies for Empowering Students' Progress

Strategy	Description	Example
Giving credit	Attributing desired changes to the student's choices and actions	"How did you decide to do that?"; "How did you make these changes?"
Exploring the personal and social effects of improvements	Inviting students to reflect on and describe how their school improvements have impacted them personally and socially	"How is the 'new you' different than the 'old you'?"; "What have you learned about yourself in making these changes?"; "How do your teachers and parents treat you differently?"
Enlisting students as consultants	Asking students for advice in helping others who are struggling with similar problems	"What would you tell other students who want to improve their school behavior?"
Exploring students' intentions to maintain progress	Inviting students to reflect on and describe their intentions and plans to sustain progress	"Do you plan to continue these changes?"; "What can you do to keep things moving in the right direction?"
Preparing for setbacks	Explaining that setbacks are a normal part of the change process and developing strategies for handling them	"What can you do if you start getting in trouble in one of your classes again?"
Offering follow-up services	Offering follow-up contacts with students after goals have been met and formal meetings are discontinued	"I'd like to check in with you now and then to see how things are going. Is that okay with you?"

2. List and briefly describe four strategies for empowering progress during interviews with students. Pair up and practice two of these strategies by conducting a short interview with your partner about a recent change that he or she has made. Switch roles and repeat the exercise.

3. Giving students ample credit for school improvements helps them to maintain such improvements. List two questions that you can use to give students credit by helping them connect positive changes to their own efforts and actions.

4. Explain why is it useful for students to reflect on and describe the personal and social benefits of school progress. List three questions that invite students to reflect on and describe the personal and social benefits of school improvements.

5. Think of a student you are currently working with who has made positive changes at school, even if the changes are small. What could you do or say that would help to enlist the student as a consultant or advisor to other students?

6. When students make positive changes at school, we can explore their plans and intentions to sustain their progress. To gain a more personalized perspective of this strategy, think about a positive change that you have recently made and ask yourself the following questions: (a) do you intend to continue these changes?; (b) how will you do that?; and (c) what will help you stick with your plans?

8. Pair up and have one person take the role of client with the other person as the counselor. Practice the following two aspects of helping people prepare for slips: (a) describe to the client how the change process often proceeds in a nonlinear way and that slips are a common part of the process; and (b) explore what the client can do to prepare for and respond to future slips. Switch roles and repeat the exercise.

9. Describe one small step that you are willing to take in your work with students as a result of the information in this chapter.

Epilogue

When a person finds her own voice, she takes charge of her own story.
—Alan Parry

I want to tell you a quick story adapted from Shah (1983). A man named Andre was walking the neighborhood one evening when he saw his friend David crawling around on his hands and knees looking for something under the streetlamp. "I lost my keys," David explained. Being a kind sort, Andre immediately joined his friend in the search for the missing keys. After a couple of minutes and still no keys, Andre asked David to think very carefully about where he was when he lost them. "I was over there," David said while pointing to a large field across the street.Puzzled by his friend's response, Andre asked the obvious question: "If you dropped your keys all the way over there, then why are you looking for them here?" Without hesitating or looking up from the ground, David said, "Because the light is so much better here."

Many interviewing approaches follow David's lead by continuing to search for school solutions under the familiar light of diagnosis despite a growing body of research indicating that the keys to solutions are more likely to be found, of all places, in the students themselves. Students' strengths, successes, values, dreams, perceptions, life experiences, cultural traditions, wisdom, feedback, and other natural resources play a much larger role in solutions than diagnostic information about the problem. The principles and practices of this book are designed to engage the most vital element of all in building school solutions—student involvement.

Most books talk about successes, and this one is no exception. Success stories inspire and encourage—two things I had hoped to do with this book. But, no single set of ideas and techniques, including those in this book, work for every student. We all have favorite theories and methods—and that's fine—as long as we are willing to part with them when they are not working for the person sitting across from us.

What better way to end a book than to talk about beginnings. Effective interviewing begins with our attitudes about students, problems, and solutions. The most successful school practitioners have faith in the helping process and in the ability of students to contribute to their own care.

I offer three parting thoughts to keep in mind as you host solution-building conversations with students in your setting.

You can't rearrange the furniture unless you are invited into the house. Relationships are vital. Our effectiveness rests largely on the extent to which students invite us inside their house and allow us to stay there—and the surest way to get invited inside is to listen to students and take them seriously. Students need to be heard, validated, and respected if we expect them to invest and involve themselves in building solutions.

Those who are closest to the problem are also closest to the solution. No one is closer to school problems than the students who experience them. Regardless of how insightful or caring we may be, students are always closer to the problem and solution than we are. That is why their perceptions and preferences are more important than ours or anyone else's when it comes to selecting, implementing, and evaluating interventions. If we want students to cooperate with us, then we need to cooperate with them.

The way we view students is a matter of choice, not fact. Some views are more useful than others when it comes to helping people change. Instead of viewing students from a diagnostic and problem-focused perspective—a perspective that often diminishes our hope and theirs—we can see them as resourceful, capable contributors to their own solutions. Without denying the pain and frustration of serious problems, student-driven interviewing invites students to assume an active role in building solutions from what is right and what is working in their lives. This approach enables us to "lift students up"—a highly valued motive for many school practitioners.

Of all the things that make practitioners successful, the most important one is that they allow themselves to be shaped into effectiveness by the people they serve. I began the book with a dedication to the greatest teachers of all—the students who have taught me how to be useful to them. Some lessons have been more difficult than others depending on my willingness to listen and learn. I have attempted to share these lessons in previous chapters, and I appreciate the time and energy you have invested in this book. Most of all, I hope it will help you serve students in respectful and useful ways.

Appendix A

Overview of Developmental Features and Accommodations

	Early Childhood (4–6 years)	Middle Childhood (7–10 years)	Early Adolescence (11–14 years)	Mid-Adolescence (15–18 years)
Physical	Substantial motor development • Take a walk • Use chairs that move • Incorporate games and art activities • Use hands-on props and materials	Control and coordination of muscles • Watch for small muscle control in handwriting • Be aware of early signs of puberty	Puberty • Expect some typical concerns about physical appearance • Be aware of rapid physical growth and changes	Continuation of physical changes • Acknowledge concerns and questions about physical appearance
Social	Social play • Integrate role-playing activities • Acknowledge likes and dislikes about school	Increased social activities • Expect and acknowledge increased power of peers	Desire for social acceptance • Acknowledge the interplay between individual and social needs	Importance of peers • Be open to discussing friendships and gender identification issues

	• Play games	• Invite active participation in the conversation	• Identify and utilize influential peers	
Psychological	Development of distinct identity • Identify unique strengths, interests, and talents • Allow for imagination and creativity in the conversation	Increased awareness of others • Expect students to compare themselves to peers • Appeal to students' internal locus of control • Encourage responsibility and account-ability for actions	Wide variations in mood and self-esteem • Expect some "magical thinking," feelings of invincibility, mood swings, and risk-taking • Acknowledge students' suspicion and distrust of adults • Compliment students on strengths and successes	More enduring and stable patterns of self-identity • Validate ambivalence and distress about the future • Openly discuss goals and values • Expect a strong commitment to independence • Work within students' frame of reference
Intellectual	Use clear, jargon-free language • Discuss the future in literal, concrete ways • Use creative questions that capture students' interest and imagination	Increased abstract thinking • Invite students to consider the impact of behavior on others • Continue to use clear and simple language	Growing ability to think in complex, abstract ways • Have students describe the future and how they can influence it	Increased ability to participate in complex discussions • Explore students' deepest values • Identify connections between big values and school performance

Appendix B

Outcome and Session Rating Scales

Outcome Rating Scale (ORS)

Name:_____ Age: ____ Session #: _____ Date: _____

Looking back over the last week, including today, help us understand how you have been feeling by rating how well you have been doing in the following areas of your life, where marks to the left represent low levels and marks to the right indicate high levels.

EXAMINATION COPY ONLY

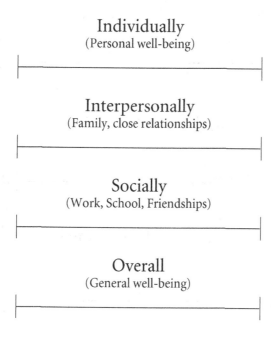

Individually
(Personal well-being)

Interpersonally
(Family, close relationships)

Socially
(Work, School, Friendships)

Overall
(General well-being)

Session Rating Scale (SRS V.3.0)

Name:_____ Age: _____ Session #: _____ Date: _____

Please rate today's session by placing a hash mark on the line nearest to the description that best fits your experience.

EXAMINATION COPY ONLY

Relationship

| I did not feel heard, understood, and respected. | ├————————————┤ | I felt heard, understood, and respected. |

Goals and Topics

| We did not work on or talk about what I wanted to work on or talk about. | ├————————————┤ | We worked on and talked about what I wanted to work on and talk about. |

Approach or Method

| The therapist's approach is not a good fit for me. | ├————————————┤ | The therapist's approach is a good fit for me. |

Overall

| There was something missing in the session today. | ├————————————┤ | Overall, today's session was right for me. |

Heart & Soul of Change Project (www.heartandsoulofchange.com)
© 2000, Lynn D. Johnson, Scott D. Miller, and Barry L. Duncan

Child Outcome Rating Scale (CORS)

Name:_____ Age: ____ Session #: _____ Date: _____

How are you doing? How are things going in your life? Please make a mark on the scale to let us know. The closer the smiley face, the better things are. The closer the frowny face, things are not so good.

EXAMINATION COPY ONLY

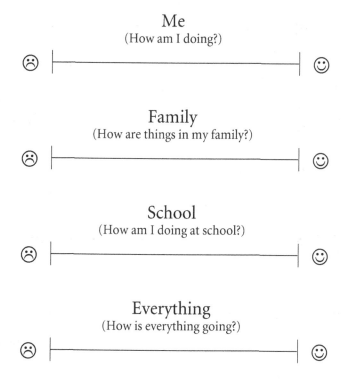

Me
(How am I doing?)

Family
(How are things in my family?)

School
(How am I doing at school?)

Everything
(How is everything going?)

Child Session Rating Scale (CSRS)

Name:_____ Age: ____ Session #: _____ Date: _____

How was our time together today? Please put a mark on the lines below to let us know how you feel.

EXAMINATION COPY

Listening

Did not always listen to me. ☹ |————————————| ☺ Listened to me.

How Important

What we did and talked about were not really that important to me. ☹ |————————————| ☺ What we did and talked about were important to me.

What We Did

I did not like what we did today. ☹ |————————————| ☺ I liked what we did today.

Overall

I wish we could do something different. ☹ |————————————| ☺ I hope we do the same kind of things next time.

Heart & Soul of Change Project (www.heartandsoulofchange.com)
© 2003, Barry L. Duncan, Scott D. Miller, Jacqueline A. Sparks, and Lynn D. Johnson

Appendix C

Tips and Scripts for Using the Outcome and Session Rating Scales with Students

Student involvement is the key to school solutions, and one of the best ways to involve students is to obtain their feedback at every meeting. This appendix provides a brief overview on how to use the two ultra brief feedback scales displayed in Appendix B—the Outcome Rating Scale (ORS) and Session Rating Scale (SRS) and their child versions (CORS and CSRS)—to assess students' perceptions of outcome (progress) and alliance (relationship) on an ongoing basis. The ORS is administered at the beginning of every session and the SRS is administered at the end.

Introducing the ORS (Ages 13 and up) or CORS (Ages 5–12) in the Beginning of the First Meeting

Here are a couple of examples of how practitioners can introduce the ORS and CORS to students.

Introducing the ORS to an older student: "As I was saying a few minutes ago when we talked about how the counseling would work, I need your help on a couple of short forms that tell me how things are going for you and how our meetings are working. This form (pointing to the ORS) tells me how you're doing in different parts of your life. Can you help me with that?"

Introducing the CORS to a younger student: "Here's the paper I mentioned earlier that I need your help on. I need you to make a mark on the line that tells me how things are going for you in these different areas like school and family and the others. There are smiley and frowny faces on each end of the line, so marks on this end (pointing to the frowny face and the left portion of the line) mean that things are not going too good for you, and marks on this end (pointing to the smiley face and the right portion of the line) mean that things are going pretty good. Can you give it a try?"

Discussing ORS or CORS Ratings

In discussing results with a student, you could say, "From your ORS, it looks like you're having some real problems"; "Your total score is 15. Things must be pretty tough for you. What's going on?"; or "From your score, it looks like you're doing okay. Why do you think you were referred for counseling?"

When discussing a particular scale on the ORS or CORS, you could say, "This mark tells me that you're really having a tough time. Can you tell me about that?" If all the marks are to the far right, you could say, "When people make their marks so far to the right like you did, it usually means things are going really well for them. Is that true for you?"

In many cases, practitioners will need to help students (a) connect their experience with their ORS marks and (b) consider what needs to happen to make things better. Here is a quick example:

"I need your help to understand what this mark [pointing to a mark on one of the ORS lines] means in your life. Does the stress from missing your older brother [or from your relationship with your father, from anxiety about taking tests, etc.] explain your mark on this line? What needs to happen for that mark to move just a little to the right?"

Introducing the SRS (Ages 13 and up) or CSRS (Ages 5–12) at the End of the First Meeting

Introducing the SRS to an older student: "I need your help on this form that tells me how our meeting went for you. It's like taking the temperature of our meeting today. Your feedback will help me stay on track and be useful to you. Will you help me by filling out the form?"

Introducing the CSRS to a younger student: "Before we stop, I want to ask you to fill out another form that has faces on it. This one deals with how you think I am doing. That's right—you get to grade me! Can you help me out with this and let me know how our visit went for you?"

Discussing SRS or CSRS Ratings

When SRS/CSRS results are uniformly high (9.0 or above in each category), the practitioner can simply acknowledge this and invite any other comments or suggestions from the student. Since people tend to rate alliance measures highly, the practitioner should address any hint of a problem on the SRS/CSRS. Anything less than a total score of 36 (or under 9 in any area) may signal a concern and warrant discussion. Here are a couple of examples:

Responding to higher SRS/CSRS ratings: "Okay, these marks are way over here to the right, which suggests that we're on the same page, that we are talking about things that are important to you, and that today's meeting was right for you. Please let me know if I get off track at any point during our work together, okay?"

Responding to lower SRS/CSRS ratings: "Let me see how you think we are doing. Okay, it seems like I am missing the boat somewhere here. Thanks for being honest and giving me a chance to change things to make it work better for you. Was there something else I should have asked about or done to make this meeting better for you? What was missing here?"

The practitioner's nondefensive acceptance of alliance problems and willingness to make adjustments speak volumes to the student and usually turn things around quickly. The SRS provides a practical and systematic way to address emerging problems in the relationship before they reach a point of no return.

Later Meetings

ORS scores serve as discussion prompts to engage students in discussing their progress and future plans. When scores increase from one meeting to the next—even if it's just a small increase—practitioners can give students credit for the change and explore their role in it, as well as using other methods to empower progress as discussed in Chapter 11.

Responding to increases in ORS/CORS scores: "Wow, your total score went up 8 whole points in one week. That's a big jump! What have you done differently to make things so much better? What will it take to keep it going? What has this taught you about yourself?"

Responding to decreases or no change in ORS/CORS scores: "Okay, so things haven't changed since the last time we talked. What do you make of that? Should we be doing something different here, or should we just hang in there and see if things change next week?"

Responding to consecutively low ORS scores: "These scores suggest that we need to try something pretty different to make things better. What could you do that might be really different—different enough to make a difference?"

Responding to consecutively low SRS scores: "These scores haven't changed for the past 2 weeks. If our meetings aren't helping, I wonder what I can do—or what we can do in these meetings—to shake things up and try something different. What do you think?"

Final Comments

Integrating the ORS and SRS into everyday practice has been shown to dramatically improve the effectiveness of practitioners (Gillaspy & Murphy, 2012). Collecting feedback—and adjusting services based on such feedback—gives students an active role in their own care and increases their involvement in building solutions. Gathering feedback does not ensure our success with every student, but it does give us a better chance to detect and correct problems before they reach a point of no return. The best thing we can do for students is to be useful. Collecting feedback helps us to do just that. Refer to Murphy and Duncan (2007) for more information about using the ORS and SRS in schools, and visit www.heartand soulofchange.com for more information on these instruments.

References

Ambady, N., & Skowronski, J. J. (Eds.). (2008). *First impressions.* New York, NY: Guilford.

American Psychological Association Task Force on Evidence-Based Practice. (2006). Evidence-based practice in psychology. *American Psychologist, 61,* 271–285.

Anker, M. G., Duncan, B. L., & Sparks, J. A. (2009). Using client feedback to improve couple therapy outcomes: A randomized clinical trial in a naturalistic setting. *Journal of Consulting and Clinical Psychology, 77,* 693–704.

Asay, T. P., & Lambert, M. J. (1999). The empirical case for the common factors in therapy: Quantitative findings. In M. A. Hubble, B. L. Duncan, & S. D. Miller (Eds.), *The heart and soul of change: What works in therapy* (pp. 33–56). Washington, DC: American Psychological Association.

Bandura, A. (2006). Toward a psychology of human agency. *Perspectives on Psychological Science, 1,* 164–180.

Benish, S. G., Imel, Z. E., & Wampold, B. E. (2008). The relative efficacy of bona fide psychotherapies for treating posttraumatic stress disorder: A meta-analysis of direct comparisons. *Clinical Psychology Review, 28,* 746–758.

Bohart, A. C., & Tallman, K. (2010). Clients: The neglected common factor in therapy. In B. L. Duncan, S. D. Miller, B. E. Wampold, & M. A. Hubble (Eds.), *The heart and soul of change: Delivering what works in therapy* (2nd ed., pp. 83–11). Washington, DC: American Psychological Association.

Boyd-Franklin, N. (2003). *Black families in therapy: Understanding the African-American experience.* New York, NY: Guilford.

Brom, D., Pat-Horenczyk, R., & Ford, J. D. (Eds.). (2009). *Treating traumatized children: Risk, resilience, and recovery.* New York, NY: Routledge.

Cantwell, P., & Holmes, S. (1994). Social construction: A paradigm shift for systemic therapy and training. *The Australian and New Zealand Journal of Family Therapy, 15,* 17–26.

Constantino, M. J., & DeGeorge, J. (2008). Believing is seeing: Clinical implications of research on patient expectations. *Psychotherapy Bulletin, 43,* 1–6.

Constantino, M. J., Glass, C. R., Arnkoff, D. B., Ametrano, R. M., & Smith, J. Z. (2011).

Expectations. In J. C. Norcross (Ed.), *Psychotherapy relationships that work: Evidence-based responsiveness* (2nd ed., pp. 354–376). New York, NY: Oxford University Press.

Crethar, H. C., Torres Rivera, E., & Nash, S. (2008). In search of common threads: Linking multicultural, feminist, and social justice counseling paradigms. *Journal of Counseling and Development, 86*, 269–278.

de Shazer, S. (1985). *Keys to solution in brief therapy.* New York, NY: Norton.

de Shazer, S. (1988). *Clues: Investigating solutions in brief therapy.* New York, NY: Norton.

de Shazer, S., Dolan, Y., Korman, H., Trepper, T., McCollum, E., & Berg, I. K. (2007). *More than miracles: The state of the art of solution-focused brief therapy.* New York, NY: Haworth Press.

Dempsey, I., & Dunst, C. (2004). Helpgiving styles and parent empowerment in families with a young child with a disability. *Journal of Intellectual & Developmental Disability, 29*, 40–51.

Dennis, M., Godley, S., Diamond, G., Tims, F., Babor, T., Donaldson, J., … Funk, R. (2004). The cannabis youth treatment (CYT) study: Main findings from two randomized trials. *Journal of Substance Abuse Treatment, 27*, 97–213.

Duncan, B. L. (2010). *On becoming a better therapist.* Washington, DC: American Psychological Association.

Duncan, B. (2012). The Partners for Change Outcome Management System (PCOMS): The heart and soul of change project. *Canadian Psychology, 53*, 93–104.

Duncan, B., Miller, S., & Sparks, J. (2003). *Child Outcome Rating Scale.* Chicago, IL: Authors.

Duncan, B., Miller, S., & Sparks, J. (2004). *The heroic client: A radical way to improve effectiveness through client-directed, outcome-informed therapy.* San Francisco, CA: Jossey-Bass.

Duncan, B. L., Miller, S. D., Sparks, J. A., & Johnson, L. D. (2003). *Child Session Rating Scale.* Ft. Lauderdale, FL: Authors.

Dunst, C. J., Boyd, K., Trivette, C. M., & Hamby, D. W. (2002). Family-oriented program models and professional help giving practices. *Family Relations, 51*, 221–229.

Duvall, J., & Béres, L. (2011). *Innovations in narrative therapy: Connecting practice, training, and research.* New York, NY: W. W. Norton.

Egan, G. (2010). *The skilled helper: A problem-management and opportunity-development approach to helping* (9th ed.). Pacific Grove, CA: Brooks/Cole.

Fisch, R., & Schlanger, K. (1999). *Brief therapy with intimidating cases: Changing the unchangeable.* San Francisco, CA: Jossey-Bass.

Fisch, R., Weakland, J. H., & Segal, L. (1982). *The tactics of change: Doing therapy briefly.* San Francisco, CA: Jossey-Bass.

Fiske, S. T., & Taylor, S. E. (2008). *Social cognition: From brains to culture.* New York, NY: McGraw-Hill.

Frank, J. D., & Frank, J. B. (1991). *Persuasion and healing* (3rd ed.). Baltimore, MD: Johns Hopkins.

Franklin, C., Trepper, T. S., Gingerich, W. J., & McCollum, E. E. (Eds.). (2012). *Solution-focused brief therapy: Research, practice, and training.* New York, NY: Oxford University Press.

Fulghum, R. (2003). *All I really need to know I learned in kindergarten.* New York, NY: Random House.

Gassman, D., & Grawe, K. (2006). General change mechanisms: The relation between problem activation and resource activation in successful and unsuccessful therapeutic interactions. *Clinical Psychology and Psychotherapy, 13*, 1–11.

Gelso, C. J., & Carter, J. A. (1994). Components of the psychotherapy relationship: Their interaction and unfolding during treatment. *Journal of Counseling Psychology, 41*, 296–306.

Gergen, K. (2009). *An invitation to social construction.* London, England: Sage.

Gillaspy, J. A., & Murphy, J. J. (2012). Incorporating outcome and session rating scales in solution-focused brief therapy. In C. Franklin, T. S. Trepper, W. J. Gingerich, & E. E. McCollum (Eds.), *Solution-focused brief therapy: Research, practice, and training* (pp.73–93).New York, NY: Oxford University Press.

Gilman, R., Huebner, E. S., & Furlong, M. J. (2009). *Handbook of positive psychology in schools.* New York, NY: Routledge.

Goldstein, A. P., & Martens, B. K. (2000). *Lasting change: Methods for enhancing generalization of gain.* Champaign, IL: Research Press.

Halvorson, H. G. (2010). *Succeed: How we can reach our goals.* New York, NY: Penguin Books.

Hannan, C., Lambert, M. J., Harmon, C., Nielsen, S. L., Smart, D. W., Shimokawa, K., & Sutton, S. W. (2005). A lab test and algorithms for identifying clients at risk for treatment failure. *Journal of Clinical Psychology: In Session, 61,* 155–163.

Harmon, S. C., Lambert, M. J., Smart, D. W., Hawkins, E. J., Nielsen, S. L., Slade, K., & Lutz, W. (2007). Enhancing outcome for potential treatment failures: Therapist/client feedback and clinical support tools. *Psychotherapy Research, 17,* 379–392.

Henderson, N., Benard, B., & Sharp-Light, N. (Eds.). (2007). *Resiliency in action: Practical ideas for overcoming risks and building strengths in youth, families, and communities.* Ojai, CA: Resiliency in Action.

Horvath, A. O., Del Re, A. C., Flückiger, C., & Symonds, D. (2011). Alliance in individual psychotherapy. In J. C. Norcross (Ed.), *Psychotherapy relationships that work: Evidence-based responsiveness* (2nd ed., pp. 25–69). New York, NY: Oxford University Press.

Imel, Z. E., & Wampold, B. E. (2008). The common factors of psychotherapy. In S. D. Brown & R. W. Lent (Eds.), *Handbook of counseling psychology* (4th ed., pp. 249–256). New York, NY: Wiley.

Ivey, A. E., & Ivey, M. B. (2008). *Essentials of intentional interviewing: Counseling in a multicultural world.* Belmont, CA: Thomson.

Johnson, C., Ironsmith, M., Snow, C., & Poteat, G. (2000). Peer acceptance and social adjustment in preschool and kindergarten. *Early Childhood Education Journal, 27,* 207–212.

Johnson, L. D., Miller, S. D., & Duncan, B. L. (2000). *Session Rating Scale 3.0.* Chicago, IL: Authors.

Karver, M. S., Handelsman, J. B., Fields, S., & Bickman, L. (2006). Meta-analysis of therapeutic relationship variables in youth and family therapy: The evidence for different relationship variables in the child and adolescent treatment outcome literature. *Clinical Psychology Review, 26,* 50–65.

Kazdin, A. E. (2007). Systematic evaluation to improve the quality of patient care: From hope to hopeful. *Pragmatic Case Studies in Psychotherapy, 3,* 37–49.

Kazdin, A. E., Marciano, P. L., & Whitley, M. K. (2005). The therapeutic alliance in cognitive-behavioral treatment of children referred for oppositional, aggressive, and antisocial behavior. *Journal of Consulting and Clinical Psychology, 73,* 726–730.

Kelly, M. S., Kim, J. S., & Franklin, C. (2008). *Solution-focused brief therapy in schools.* Oxford, England: Oxford University Press.

Kindsvater, A. (2007). Factors associated with counseling client perceptions of contributions to pre-treatment change. *Dissertation Abstracts International, 67,* 4108.

Kirsch, I. (2010). *The emperor's new drugs: Exploding the antidepressant myth.* New York, NY: Basic Books.

Lambert, M. J. (2008, June). *The stunning benefits of client feedback on outcome.* Paper presented at the Heart and Soul of Change Conference, Phoenix, AZ.

Lambert, M. J. (2010). "Yes, it is time for clinicians to routinely monitor treatment outcome." In B. L. Duncan, S. D. Miller, B. E. Wampold, & M. A. Hubble (Eds.), *The heart and soul of change: Delivering what works in therapy* (2nd ed., pp. 239–266). Washington, DC: American Psychological Association.

Lambert, M. J., & Ogles, B. (2004). The efficacy and effectiveness of psychotherapy. In M. J. Lambert (Ed.), *Bergin and Garfield's handbook of psychotherapy and behavior change* (5th ed., pp. 39–193). New York, NY: Wiley.

Lambert, M. J., & Shimokawa, (2011). Collecting client feedback. In J. C. Norcross (Ed.), *Psychotherapy relationships that work: Evidence-based responsiveness* (2nd ed., pp. 203–223). New York, NY: Oxford University Press.

Linssen, F., & Kerzbeck, U. (2002, September). *Does solution-focused therapy work?* Paper presented at the meeting of the European Brief Therapy Association, Cardiff, Wales.

Lippke, S., Wiedemann, A. U., Ziegelmann, J. P., Reuter, T., & Schwarzer, R. (2009). Self-efficacy moderates the mediation of intentions into behavior via plans. *American Journal of Health Behavior, 33*, 521–529.

Mackrill, T. (2008). Pre-treatment change in psychotherapy with adult children of problem drinkers: The significance of leaving home. *Counseling and Psychotherapy Research, 8*, 160–165.

MacMartin, C. (2008). Resisting optimistic questions in narrative and solution-focused therapies. In A. Perakyla, C. Antaki, S. Vehvilainen, & I. Leuder (Eds.), *Conversational analysis and psychotherapy* (pp. 80–99). New York, NY: Cambridge University Press.

Margolis, H., & McCabe, P. (2006). Motivating struggling readers in an era of mandated instructional practices. *Reading Psychology, 27*, 435–455.

Martin, J., Romas, M., Medford, M., Leffert, N., & Hatcher, S. L. (2006). Adult helping qualities preferred by adolescents. *Adolescence, 41*, 127–140.

Masten, A. (2001). Ordinary magic: Resilience processes in development. *American Psychologist, 56*, 227–238.

Mayall, B. (2002). *The sociology of childhood*. Philadelphia, PA: Open University Press.

McAuliffe, G., & Associates. (2013). *Culturally alert counseling: A comprehensive introduction* (2nd ed.). Thousand Oaks, CA: Sage.

McGuinness, T. M. (2008). Hate crime 101: Making the world (and school) safe for GLBT youth. *Journal of Psychosocial Nursing & Mental Health Services, 46*, 8–9.

McGuire, W. J., & McGuire, C. V. (1996). Enhancing self-esteem by directed-thinking tasks: Cognitive and affective positivity asymmetries. *Journal of Personality and Social Psychology, 70*, 1117–1125.

Meier, S. T., & Davis, S. R. (2011). *The elements of counseling* (7th ed.). Belmont, CA: Brooks/Cole.

Miller, S. D., & Duncan, B. L. (2000). *Outcome Rating Scale*. Chicago, IL: Author.

Miller, S. D., Duncan, B. L., Brown, J., Sorrell, R., & Chalk, M. B. (2006). Using outcome to inform and improve treatment outcomes. *Journal of Brief Therapy, 5*, 26–36.

Miller, S. D., Duncan, B. L., Brown, J., Sparks, J., & Claud, D. (2003). The outcome rating scale: A preliminary study of the reliability, validity, and feasibility of a brief visual analog measure. *Journal of Brief Therapy, 2*, 91–100.

Miller, S. D., Wampold, B. E., & Varhely, K. (2008). Direct comparisons of treatment modalities for childhood disorders: A meta-analysis. *Psychotherapy Research, 18*, 5–14.

Molden, D. C., & Dweck, C. S. (2006). Finding "meaning" in psychology: A lay theories approach to self-regulation, social perception, and social development. *American Psychologist, 61*, 192–203.

Mozak, H. H., & Maniacci, M. P. (2008). Adlerian psychotherapy. In R. J. Corsini & D. Wedding (Eds.), *Current psychotherapies* (8th ed., pp. 63–106). Belmont, CA: Brooks/Cole.

Murphy, J. J. (2008). *Solution-focused counseling in schools* (2nd ed.). Alexandria, VA: American Counseling Association.

Murphy, J. J. (2010). Therapist as travel agent. In B. Duncan & J. Sparks (Eds.), *Heroic clients, heroic agencies: Partners for change* (2nd ed., pp. 205–227). Jensen Beach, FL: Author.

Murphy, J. J., & Duncan, B. L. (2007). *Brief intervention for school problems: Outcome-informed strategies* (2nd ed.). New York, NY: Guilford.

Ness, M. E., & Murphy, J. J. (2001). The effect of inquiry technique on reports of pretreatment change by clients in a university counseling center. *Journal of College Counseling, 4*, 20–31.

Norcross, J. C. (2010). The therapeutic relationship. In B. L. Duncan, S. D. Miller, B. E. Wampold, & M. A. Hubble (Eds.), *The heart and soul of change: Delivering what works in therapy* (2nd ed., pp. 113–141). Washington, DC: American Psychological Association.

Norcross, J. C. (Ed.). (2011). *Psychotherapy relationships that work: Evidence-based responsiveness* (2nd ed.). New York, NY: Oxford University Press.

O'Hanlon, W. H., & Bertolino, B. (2002). *Even from a broken web: Brief, respectful solution-oriented therapy for sexual abuse and trauma.* New York, NY: Norton.

O'Hanlon, W. H., & Weiner-Davis, M. (2003). *In search of solutions: A new direction in psychotherapy* (2nd ed.). New York, NY: Norton.

Orlinsky, D. E., Rønnestad, M. H., & Willutzki, U. (2004). Fifty years of psychotherapy process-outcome research: Continuity and change. In M. J. Lambert (Ed.), *Bergin and Garfield's handbook of psychotherapy and behavior change* (5th ed., pp. 307–389). New York, NY: Wiley.

Parsons, R. D., & Kahn, W. J. (2005). *The school counselor as consultant.* Belmont, CA: Brooks/Cole.

Price, D. P., Finniss, D. F., & Benedetti, F. (2008). A comprehensive review of the placebo effect: Recent advances and current thought. *Annual Review of Psychology, 59*, 565–590.

Reese, R. J., Nosworthy, L., & Rowlands, S. (2009). Does a continuous feedback system improve psychotherapy outcomes? *Psychotherapy, 46*, 418–431.

Ridley, C. R. (2005). *Overcoming unintentional racism in counseling and therapy: A practitioner's guide to intentional intervention* (2nd ed.). Thousand Oaks, CA: Sage.

Rollnick, S., Miller, W. R., & Butler, C. C. (2008). *Motivational interviewing in health care.* New York, NY: Guilford.

Seligman, M. E. (2011). *Flourish: A visionary new understanding of happiness and well-being.* New York, NY: Free Press.

Seligman, M. E. P., Rashid, T., & Parks, A. C. (2006). Positive psychotherapy. *American Psychologist, 61*, 774–788.

Shah, I. (1983). *The exploits of the incomparable Mulla Nasrudin.* London, England: Octagon Press.

Shapiro, J. P., Friedberg, R. D., & Bardenstein, K. K. (2006). *Child and adolescent therapy: Science and art.* New York, NY: Wiley.

Shirk, S. R., & Karver, M. S. (2003). Prediction of treatment outcome from relationship variables in child and adolescent therapy: A meta-analytic review. *Journal of Consulting and Clinical Psychology, 71*, 452–464.

Shirk, S. R., & Karver, M. S. (2011). Alliance in child and adolescent psychotherapy. In J. C. Norcross (Ed.), *Psychotherapy relationships that work: Evidence-based responsiveness* (2nd ed., pp. 70–91). New York, NY: Oxford University Press.

Shirk, S. R., Karver, M. S., & Brown, R. (2011). The alliance in child and adolescent psychotherapy. *Psychotherapy, 48*, 17–24.

Short, D., Erickson, B. A., & Erickson-Klein, R. (2005). *Hope and resiliency: Understanding the psychotherapeutic strategies of Milton H. Erickson.* Norwalk, CT: Crown House.

Sigelman, C. K., & Rider, E. A. (2012). *Life-span human development* (7th ed.). Belmont, CA: Wadsworth.

Snyder, C. R., Lopez, S. J., & Pedrotti, J. T. (2011). *Positive psychology: The scientific and practical exploration of human strengths* (2nd ed.). Thousand Oaks, CA: Sage.

Snyder, C. R., Lopez, S. J., Shorey, H. S., Rand, K. L., & Feldman, D. B. (2003). Hope theory, measurements, and applications to school psychology. *School Psychology Quarterly, 18*, 122–139.

Snyder, C. R., Michael, S. T., & Cheavens, J. S. (1999). Hope as a psychotherapeutic foundation of common factors, placebos, and expectancies. In M. A. Hubble, B. L. Duncan, & S. D. Miller (Eds.), *The heart and soul of change* (pp. 179–200). Washington, DC: American Psychological Association.

Spielmans, G. I., Pasek, L. F., & McFall, J. P. (2007). What are the active ingredients in cognitive and behavioral psychotherapy for anxious and depressed children? A meta-analytic review. *Clinical Psychology Review, 27*, 642–654.

Sprenkle, D. H., Davis, S. D., & Lebow, J. L. (2009). *Common factors in couple and family therapy*. New York, NY: Guilford Press.

Sue, D. W., & Sue, D. (2013). *Counseling the culturally diverse: Theory and practice* (6th ed.). New York, NY: Wiley.

Tryon, G. S., Collins, S., & Felleman, E. (2006, August). *Meta-analysis of the third session client-therapist working alliance*. Paper presented at the annual meeting of the American Psychological Association, New Orleans, LA.

Tryon, G. S., & Winograd, G. (2011). Goal consensus and collaboration. In J. C. Norcross (Ed.), *Psychotherapy relationships that work: Evidence-based responsiveness* (2nd ed., pp. 153–167). New York, NY: Oxford University Press.

Van Houten, R., Van Houten, J., & Louis Malenfant, J. E. (2007). Impact of a comprehensive safety program on bicycle helmet use among middle-school children. *Journal of Applied Behavior Analysis, 40*, 239–247.

Vera, E. M., & Reese, L. E. (2000). Prevention interventions with school-age youth. In S. D. Brown & R. W. Lent (Eds.), *Handbook of counseling psychology* (3rd ed., pp. 411–434). New York, NY: Wiley.

Wampold, B. E. (2001). *The great psychotherapy debate: Models, methods, and findings*. Mahwah, NJ: Erlbaum.

Wampold, B. E. (2010). The research evidence for the common factors models: A historically situated perspective. In B. L. Duncan, S. D. Miller, B. E. Wampold, & M. A. Hubble (Eds.), *The heart and soul of change: Delivering what works in therapy* (2nd ed., pp. 49–81). Washington, DC: American Psychological Association.

Watson, T. S., & Steege, M. W. (2009). *Conducting school-based functional behavioral assessments* (2nd ed.). New York, NY: Guilford.

Watzlawick, P., Weakland, J., & Fisch, R. (1974). *Change: Principles of problem formation and problem resolution*. New York, NY: Norton.

Weiner-Davis, M., de Shazer, S., & Gingerich, W. (1987). Using pretreatment change to construct a therapeutic solution: An exploratory study. *Journal of Marital and Family Therapy, 13*, 359–363.

Whalley, B., Hyland, M. E., & Kirsch, I. (2008). Consistency of the placebo effect. *Journal of Psychosomatic Research, 64*, 537–541.

White, M. (2007). *Maps of narrative practice*. New York, NY: Norton.

White, M., & Epston, D. (1990). *Narrative means to therapeutic ends*. New York, NY: Norton.

Willis, J., & Todorov, A. (2006). First impressions: Making up your mind after a 100-ms exposure to a face. *Psychological Science, 17*, 592–598.

Winslade, J. M., & Monk, G. D. (2007). *Narrative counseling in schools* (2nd ed.). Thousand Oaks, CA: Corwin Press.

Wolin, S., Desetta, A., & Hefner, K. (2000). *A leader's guide to the struggle to be strong: How to foster resilience in teens*. Minneapolis, MN: Free Spirit Publishing.

Zuroff, D. C., & Blatt, S. J. (2006). The therapeutic relationship in the brief treatment of depression: Contributions to clinical improvement and enhanced adaptive capacities. *Journal of Consulting and Clinical Psychology, 74*, 130–140.

Index